About This Book

Why is this topic important?

Breakthrough communication occurs when ideas, thoughts, feelings, learning, knowledge, insights, and wisdom that might otherwise have remained dormant are allowed to emerge in an evocative but safe way. Breakthrough communication obliterates barriers and puts us in touch with ourselves and in connection with others. Imagine people deeply connecting with each other. This whole new level of communicating is a place where active listening to each other, reflecting on our experiences, and synthesizing new insights from each other's experiences are commonplace. Stories help people to communicate with one another in surprising ways. By sharing stories, we are better able to express and appreciate our differences. The social network of stories becomes the fabric for meaning to emerge. Our differentiated sets of experiences are integrated and tied together by the rich, fluid nature of stories. In this medium of stories, we create the foundation for building a true community of learners.

What can you achieve with this book?

Once Upon a Time will show you how to develop exceptional communication skills, and it will serve as an invaluable resource for helping others do the same. Stories are a natural part of how we communicate. Yet many of us are unaware of the different ways we use stories. We will take the intuitive aspects of communicating through stories and break it down into repeatable practices and essential competencies. The story-based activities in the second half of the book will give you powerful, easy to lead, structured, experiential exercises that can be used in a variety of settings and for lots of different purposes that go beyond training.

How is this book organized?

Once Upon a Time is divided into two parts. Part One of the book offers story-based techniques and tools for developing breakthrough communication. Topics covered include how stories function, what role they play in effective communication, how stories are wonderful tools for creating experiential learning, the five levels on which stories operate, and nine ground rules for working with stories. Developed from research with Fortune 500 companies, a story-based communication competency model is presented, along with a tool to measure them. Part One ends with guidelines on how to help others make sense out of their stories.

Part Two of the book is a collection of story-based activities for developing breakthrough communication skills. The introduction to Part Two provides two charts to help you select the activity best suited for your purposes. The book's table of contents will also be helpful, since it includes short descriptions of all the activities. Part Two ends with tips and techniques for telling stories, selecting stories, and "story energizers", short and fun story-based exercises for recharging a group. The CD-ROM accompanying the book includes many resources and handouts to support you.

About Pfeiffer

Pfeiffer serves the professional development and hands-on resource needs of training and human resource practitioners and gives them products to do their jobs better. We deliver proven ideas and solutions from experts in HR development and HR management, and we offer effective and customizable tools to improve workplace performance. From novice to seasoned professional, Pfeiffer is the source you can trust to make yourself and your organization more successful.

Essential Knowledge   Pfeiffer produces insightful, practical, and comprehensive materials on topics that matter the most to training and HR professionals. Our Essential Knowledge resources translate the expertise of seasoned professionals into practical, how-to guidance on critical workplace issues and problems. These resources are supported by case studies, worksheets, and job aids and are frequently supplemented with CD-ROMs, websites, and other means of making the content easier to read, understand, and use.

Essential Tools   Pfeiffer's Essential Tools resources save time and expense by offering proven, ready-to-use materials—including exercises, activities, games, instruments, and assessments—for use during a training or team-learning event. These resources are frequently offered in looseleaf or CD-ROM format to facilitate copying and customization of the material.

Pfeiffer also recognizes the remarkable power of new technologies in expanding the reach and effectiveness of training. While e-hype has often created whizbang solutions in search of a problem, we are dedicated to bringing convenience and enhancements to proven training solutions. All our e-tools comply with rigorous functionality standards. The most appropriate technology wrapped around essential content yields the perfect solution for today's on-the-go trainers and human resource professionals.

Pfeiffer
www.pfeiffer.com   *Essential resources for training and HR professionals*

Pfeiffer™

Once Upon a Time

Using Story-Based Activities to Develop Breakthrough Communication Skills

Terrence L. Gargiulo

John Wiley & Sons, Inc.

Library of Congress Cataloging-in-Publication Data

Gargiulo, Terrence L.

  Once upon a time : using story-based activities to develop breakthrough communication skills / Terrence L. Gargiulo.

    p. cm.

  ISBN-13: 978-0-7879-8535-6 (cloth)

  1. Business communication. 2. Interpersonal communication. I. Title.

  HF5718.G3675 2007

  658.4'5—dc22

                        2007007220

Acquiring Editor: Martin Delahoussaye

Director of Development: Kathleen Dolan Davies

Developmental Editor: Susan Rachmeler

Production Editor: Dawn Kilgore

Editor: Rebecca Taff

Manufacturing Supervisor: Becky Carreño

Wiley Bicentennial Logo: Richard J. Pacifico

Printed in the United States of America

Printing   10   9   8   7   6   5   4   3   2   1

Contents

> A working definition of breakthrough communication skills is offered and the contents and structure of the book are explained.

> The introduction lays out the three goals for Part One.

> This chapter presents a framework for how stories function and the role they play in communication. Stories are shown to be an excellent vehicle for creating experiential learning in any setting. An examination of the five levels that stories operate on is followed by nine ground rules for working with stories.

> Nine story-based communication competencies derived from research with Fortune 500 companies are presented. These are essential for developing breakthrough communication skills in yourself and others. The chapter provides a tool for assessing your competencies.

> This chapter shows you how to help others make sense out of their stories. A discussion of sense making with stories is followed by practical techniques for how to manage four dynamics that arise with groups when you work with stories to discover meaning.

Contents of the CD-ROM

Acknowledgments

There is always a story behind the story. As I write this, my ninety-one-year-old father nears the end of his life. I will spend my life reflecting on all of the wonderful stories he has given me. The magic I have tried to re-create in this book is a testament to his art as a conductor and composer. Exceptional facilitation of breakthrough communication is like orchestrating the intricate dynamics of a piece of music. While I have not followed in my father's path as a conductor, I feel his gifts and powers of connecting music, with the hearts of people alive and pulsing in every cell of my being. Mille grazie, Mio Padre. I will never stop trying to create something new from my being each and every moment, and you will be there always as my inspiration.

The gentle spirit deep and true of my wife, Cindy, renews my hope and gives me strength. My dear children, Gabriel and Sophia, touch my imagination. Not enough could ever be said about my mother. She has been a self-less, tireless guide. She has been with me every step of the way, showing me how to grow into myself and reach out to the world with ever greater confidence and love. My sister Franca and brother-in-law Tom are steady voices that help me stay the course and offer warm, accepting companionship. A huge, "thank you" goes out to Barry Rosen for his contribution of the *Listening as an Ally* activity and to Interaction Associates for sharing some of their knowledge and wisdom around the arts of facilitation. And to my dear friends, Hal Kane, Lin O'Neill, Robb Murray, Tom Bunzel, Angleo Ioffreda, and Jamie Douraghy, thank you for your ever-ready ears and constant encouragement.

I have been fortunate to have many wonderful mentors help me formulate my thoughts and develop my practice. I am forever grateful for Professor Luis Yglesias' initiation into the world of stories. Professor David Boje and all my colleagues at the STORI Institute in New Mexico, Grace Ann Rosile, Jo Tyler, Carolyn Gardner, Ken Baskin, and Theodore Taptiklis, are having a profound impact on my thinking and being. I look forward to participating in our growing story. I appreciate the time and care Michele Auzene spent in working with David Boje and myself on the Story-Based Communication Competency Self-Assessment Tool (SCCT).

All the incredible folks at Pfeiffer deserve a standing ovation. My editor, Martin Delahoussaye, has coaxed me, goaded me, and polished my burgeoning ideas with the patience of a saint. This is the second book for which Susan Rachmeler has acted as development editor and nurtured my words on a page into books that I am very proud of. I am very grateful for the professionalism of all the other Pfeiffer team members, including Kathleen Dolan Davies, Julie Rodriguez, Dawn Kilgore, Rebecca Taff, and Jeanenne Ray. How you keep all the details straight and exhibit such care and attention for every book is beyond me. But darn, you are good at it. Thanks are due to Marq Lee for his work on all of the title pages in Part Two of the book. I have also been inspired by the artwork of Christine de Camp.

I must end by thanking you. This is a special book to me. I sincerely believe that this book comes straight through me and my experiences to you and that it offers some very tangible and real ways to create more powerful and meaningful connections to each other. Enjoy—and please reach out to me—I want to hear your stories and learn from your journeys.

Foreword

Mel Silberman

He ran up to me at the end of a conference session, grabbed my hand, and shook it vigorously. "That was a stellar presentation, Mr. Silberman. You are an extraordinary storyteller; thank you for sharing your gift with us this afternoon." He pressed a business card into my hand and walked away before I even had to chance thank him for his comments. Later that night I emptied the contents of my pocket and found his card. Hm . . . I thought to myself, "Terrence L. Gargiulo, president of MAKINGSTORIES.net." That's interesting. I wonder what he does. That was over seven years ago. Since then I have learned quite a bit about this extraordinary facilitator.

As Terrence was preparing to write this book, he asked me whether I would be interested in working with him on the project. The link between my passions for experiential and active learning was clear, but I was at a loss as to how I could help him. He was quick to remind me, "Mel, you do this stuff all the time. You're brilliant at it, and it's so easy for you."

"Alright, Terrence, that's all well and good and thanks for the flattery, but I'm not sure if I can teach people how to do this—that's your bailiwick," I responded. "Besides, if I am an effective communicator with stories, I am completely unconscious of what I am doing and how I am doing it. Give me an example of what I do so well that you appreciate."

Never one to turn down a challenge, Terrence replied, "Okay. Do you remember the discussion you were leading last week on how to understand people during your PeopleSmart workshop?"

"Yes. . . . What about it?"

"When people were struggling with the techniques and tools you were presenting, you began to elicit people's experiences. In ten minutes you amassed this rich collection of people's stories. Without judging any of them, you probed the group with reflective questions. People started working with each other's stories and within moments connections, lessons, parallels, insights, and advice started pouring out of everyone's mouths. The energy was contagious, and the excitement in the room was unbelievable. Then you masterfully helped the group distill and organize the flood of information. The link between the workshop's material and people's day-to-day struggles with understanding other people jumped alive. You used stories to tickle their imaginations."

I was still a little puzzled by Terrence's passionate display of enthusiasm. I pressed him further, "That's an interesting observation. Tell me more."

"Look, Mel, I know this way of communicating is second-nature to you. You see stories are pervasive—they are all around us. Stories are how we communicate, learn, and think, but knowing how to leverage their power is a latent capacity that remains dormant in most of us. In order for people to experience breakthrough communication skills, this potential needs to be unleashed. That's our job. That's why I get up in the morning."

"Right now, Terrence, you are tiring me out. I think this is a project you should tackle on your own. You have my blessing, and I even promise to write a foreword for this prodigious undertaking. I can't wait to see how you craft this book." So here I am writing the foreword.

Once Upon a Time: Using Story-Based Activities to Develop Breakthrough Communication Skills serves a dual purpose: it will show you how to develop exceptional communication skills and it will serve as an invaluable resource for helping others do the same. I can't say enough about this book or the unique facilitation talents of Terrence. In my humble opinion, this book is destined to become a classic.

Introduction

Once upon a time, we were all naturally great communicators without trying or even thinking about it, and then something happened. This book unravels an overlooked and poorly understood tool we all possess. That tool is story. We live and breathe stories every moment of our lives. We take them for granted, and they certainly don't seem like they need a lot of explaining. We know what they are and we're already convinced they work, but do we know how to use them? This book will guide you in how to use story-based techniques, tools, and activities to bring people to a whole new level of communicating.

Breakthrough communication obliterates barriers and puts us in touch with ourselves and in connection with others. Imagine people deeply connecting with each other. This whole new level of communicating is a place in which active listening to each other, reflecting on our experiences, and synthesizing new insights from each other's experiences are commonplace. You see, stories help people to commune with one another in surprising ways. By sharing stories we are better able to express and appreciate our differences. The social network of stories becomes the fabric for meaning to emerge. Think of stories as complex self-organizing systems. Our differentiated sets of experiences are integrated and tied together by the rich, fluid nature of stories. In this medium of stories, we create the foundation for building a true community of learners.

I will not bore you with theories and elaborate justifications as to why stories are so important. This is a roll up your sleeves and let's gets to work kind of a book. Although the book is intended for facilitators and performance and learning professionals, it has something to offer anyone interested in developing breakthrough communication skills. It is written and organized to reach multiple audiences and, in addition to being a guide to facilitators wishing to work with stories, it can also be used for personal development and organizational interventions.

Organization of the Book

The book is divided into two parts. Part One of the book offers story-based techniques and tools for developing breakthrough communication. Chapter 1 looks at how stories function and what role they play in effective communication. We look at how stories are wonderful tools for creating experiential learning and outline five levels that stories operate on. The chapter ends with nine ground rules for working with stories. These are the essential techniques for anyone using stories with a group.

Chapter 2 presents a competency model for story-based communication that was derived from research with Fortune 500 companies. After a brief introduction to the model, a tool (Story-Based Communication Competency Tool or SCCT) for assessing your command of these competencies is offered, along with some guidance on how to interpret your results.

Chapter 3 looks at how we use stories to make sense of the world. A discussion of sense making is followed by practical techniques for how to manage four dynamics that arise when you work with stories to generate sense and meaning from them.

Part Two of the book is a collection of story-based activities for developing breakthrough communication skills. The introduction to Part Two provides two charts to help you select the activity best suited for your purposes. The book's table of contents will also be helpful, since it includes short descriptions of all the activities. Part Two ends with tips and techniques for telling stories, selecting stories, and "story energizers"—exercises that are short, fun story-based exercises for recharging a group.

Appendix A is a short article on how the power of story is in listening—a key message of this book and tenet of breakthrough communication skills. Appendix B includes sample workshop agendas to give you some ideas of how to combine the tools and activities found in the book to create powerful learning experiences for others.

The CD-ROM accompanying the book includes four audio files, a Flash file animating the story-based communication competency model discussed in Chapter 2, and lots of handouts to support you when you are running your own workshops.

Resist the urge to jump right into the activities found in Part Two of the book. There is critical information in Part One of the book. At a minimum, read Chapter 2 and use the tool in it to better understand your strengths and unique combination of story-based communication competencies.

Final Thoughts

I am thrilled to share what I have learned. When communication works well, it is a joy. Even the tough stuff becomes a soulful opportunity to enrich our understanding of our selves and others. I want this book to jumpstart your purposeful use of stories and begin a journey for you. I'd love to hear your stories, so please contact me: terrence@makingstories.net or 781–894–4381. I will find a way to pass along what you discover to others.

Communication is a fascinating phenomenon. If we could all communicate better, wouldn't it be a better world? Trite but true. And as fascinating and as important as communication is, it somehow resists our attempts to systematize and mechanize it into inscrutable practices or irrefutable principles. We are imperfect. While there are no silver bullets, stories open a whole new realm of connecting and learning from each other that otherwise remains an elusive ideal.

Part One

Story-Based Techniques and Tools for Developing Breakthrough Communication Skills

Facilitators must possess exceptional communication skills. Stories are a natural part of how we communicate. Yet many of us are unaware of the different ways we use stories. Part One of the book contains concrete techniques and tools for working with stories. We will take the intuitive aspects of communicating through stories and break them down into repeatable practices and essential competencies.

Communication is a complex phenomenon. As facilitators we help people connect better with themselves and with others. Breakthrough communication occurs when ideas, thoughts, feelings, learning, knowledge, insights, and wisdom that might have otherwise remained dormant are allowed to emerge in an evocative but safe way. We connect with ourselves and others in deeper and more meaningful ways.

Our approach to stories will be unique. Keep in mind that "storytelling" plays a minor role. Telling a story results in engaging listeners, but by itself it is only slightly better than giving people didactic facts and figures to digest. In the first three chapters we will explore how listening, reflecting, and synthesizing are essential aspects of why stories are an integral part of developing breakthrough communication skills.

Part One of the book has three goals:

1. To help you to become more aware of how to work with stories and what they can do for you as a facilitator

2. To discuss and measure the story-based communication competencies that are essential to breakthrough communication skills

3. To explore the dynamics of sense making with stories

There is a lot of information packed into these first three chapters. Once you start trying the activities in Part Two of the book, many of the concepts in Part One will come alive in a whole different way. Stories are experiential in nature. As we share them and hear them, they grace us with endless opportunities for insights and growth.

1

Techniques for Working with Stories

Stories go hand in hand with effective communication. In this chapter we begin by looking at the relationship between stories and experiential learning. Developing breakthrough communication skills in ourselves and others benefits from a synergistic relationship between the two. Next we examine a simple framework for how stories function. This is a well-established communication framework that I have developed (see my book *The Strategic Use of Stories in Organizational Communication and Learning*). It offers us a workaround to the near-impossible task of agreeing on what constitutes a story. Following the framework, we explore five levels on which stories operate. The chapter ends with nine communication ground rules and some techniques to guide us when we are working with stories.

Stories and Experiential Learning

According to the Association of Experiential Education, experiential learning is "the process through which a learner constructs knowledge, skill, and value from direct experience." Reflection is also a central part of many definitions. Experiential learning immerses us into a sea of participatory engagement with unchartered domains of knowledge. Stories possess the potential to gift us with new-found wisdom. They offer a wealth of opportunities for surfacing insights. In other words, stories are stimuli for triggering the imaginative production of engaging models of learning that can be synthesized by tellers and listeners. Stories are exciters of learning and containers of meaning that we can unpack to shed new light on ourselves.

Experiential learning occurs when we impregnate the environment with possibilities. Our stories catalyze the petri dish of learning. We are experimenting with growing new insights. Stories are used to help us stumble along old, distant, dried-up tributaries until learning flows into an ocean of new consciousness joined with the diversity of other people's knowledge and experiences. Think more in terms of drawing out people's experiences and relating these to the discussion at hand, rather than telling premeditated or orchestrated stories. Of course, you may find yourself sharing a story at a specific point during a learning event or when certain themes emerge, but experiential learning is not a public speaking event that is a rehearsed show.

Our experiences are recorded and re-examined through our stories. Stories therefore are a natural, ever-ready, ever-present tool for experiential learning. People walk around with their stories; all we need to do is elicit their stories and create a safe, supportive environment that promotes reflection. When people share their experiences, a rich playground of learning is created.

For facilitators, stories are an essential communication tool for experiential learning because they have the power to safely move participants from their comfort zones to encounter something totally new. In this way stories act as transporters. They are low-tech virtual reality simulators capable of fabricating vast intricate worlds of discovery. Every time a story is told, listeners enter the realm of the imagination. What we can imagine has the power to change who and how we are. The learning moves from being abstract to becoming imbued with vibrant potentiality. We are seduced by the realization that we can change. We do not need to be enslaved by the labels and habits of past behaviors. Change is not only possible but becomes a powerful attracting force that draws us into new ways of being.

The imagination is a sacred learning place that touches our hearts, emotions, and minds. Stories activate our imaginations. Stories offer us the opportunity to scrutinize our operating models of the world. Through stories we realize we do not have to be slaves to the perceptual filters we have constructed over time. Perceptual filters are the glasses through we view the world. They constitute an operating model of how we interpret our experiences and perceive others. We build these perceptual filters of the world from our experiences, and our experiences are stored as stories that form perceptual filters. Our behaviors are often unconsciously guided by these perceptual filters. (See Figure 1.1.) Stories are theaters of imagination whereby people can play with characters and plots to fashion new possibilities for themselves. As we become more conscious of how our experiences have built our sets of perceptual filters, we gain more control of our behaviors.

Our experiences are stored in the containers of stories. The act of remembering a story enables us to assemble parts of ourselves for greater introspection. Stories

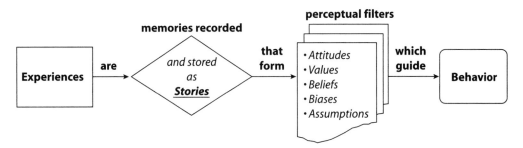

Figure 1.1. How Experiences Are Stories That Form Perceptual Filters

are vehicles for experiential learning because they allow us to tap into the wealth and variety of personal experiences and share them collectively with a group.

Stories require active listening. This is the most crucial and vital capacity of stories. It is easy to get caught up in telling stories. It's what we are the most familiar with; but telling stories just scratches the surface of why they are such effective learning tools. By its nature, learning is both a solitary and a communal phenomenon. No one can give us learning. We have to work with whatever is offered to us and turn it into something we own. Whether it be a concept, an idea, a practice, or an insight, we must use our faculties to actively take possession of it. In this way learning is solitary. However, we cannot learn in a void. We require interaction. Like molecules of water heated and bouncing off one another to create steam, our learning is accelerated by the knowledge and experiences of others.

The quickest way to share experiences is through stories. When we use stories to stimulate experiential learning, we gain the benefit of a network full of nodes rich in experiences. Our learning is driven by the correspondences between our experiences and the experiences of others. Even if the relationship between your experience and mine is not a direct one, we are still given an opportunity to reflect. Stories trigger associations, and through these associations and our reflecting on them we are invited to learn in a deep, lasting, and fundamental way.

Sharing a story with a group is a perfect opportunity to model how to work with stories in a reflective manner. Offer people a chance to react to your story. Be open to hear what others see in your story. If it triggers a story for someone, make time to hear his or her story and explore the relationship between the stories. It's not to say that you should never have a premeditated reason for sharing a story, but realize that any such intentions should only be used to jump start a process of discovery. Experiential learning invites the unexpected. The unknown epiphanies and how they happen are an essential part of stories' magic.

Nine Functions of Stories: A Framework for Understanding How Stories Work in Communication

Whenever anyone asks me for a definition of stories, I steer clear of giving one. Stories can mean lots of different things to different people. There is a whole discipline devoted to just the study of narrative. While definitions are important, I am not going to offer you one for stories. There's a lot of debate as to what is a story, and I have no wish to advocate for one definition over another. In order to leverage stories for developing breakthrough communication skills through experiential learning, it may not be important to nail down a definitive definition. From my research and experience of working with stories, I have identified some of the ways they function and how these functions are conducive to facilitating experiential learning. I have observed the following nine functions of stories, as outlined in Table 1.1.

Table 1.1. Nine Functions of Stories and Their Effects

Stories are used to:	Stories have the following effects:
1. Empower a speaker	Entertain
2. Create an environment	Create trust and openness between yourself and others
3. Bind and bond individuals	Elicit stories from others
4. Engage our minds in active listening	Listen actively in order to:
	Understand context and perspective
	Identify the root cause of a problem
	Uncover resistance and hidden agendas
	Shift perspectives in order to:
	See each other
	Experience empathy
	Enter new frames of reference
5. Negotiate differences	Hold diverse points of view
	Become aware of operating biases and values
6. Encode information	Create a working metaphor to illuminate an opinion, rationale, vision, or decision

Stories are used to:	Stories have the following effects:
7. Act as tools for thinking	Establish connections between different ideas and concepts to support an opinion or decision
8. Serve as weapons	
9. Bring about healing	Think outside the box to generate creative solutions and breakthroughs

These nine functions are essential aspects of leading any learning experience. On the surface we use stories to warm up a group, entertain them, or create an environment. When you tell a story to a group, think in terms of how it will help you set the stage and model the ground rules you wish to follow for a learning event. As a general rule of thumb, if we are a little vulnerable, circumspect, and reflective, and if we don't take ourselves too seriously, our intentions will spread through the group and positively affect its behaviors. People will also form better bonds with one another. Each story told exposes more points of connection between people.

Steer away from using stories just to encode information. Stories that encode predigested messages such as allegories or fables offer the weakest form of communication and learning. For example:

The Fox and the Lion

When a fox that had never yet seen a lion fell in with him by chance for the first time in the forest, he was so frightened that he nearly died with fear. On meeting him for the second time, he was still much alarmed, but not to the same extent as at first. On seeing him the third time, he so increased in boldness that he went up to him and commenced a familiar conversation with him. Acquaintance softens prejudices.

Source: Aesop. (1871). Three hundred Aesop's fables (trans. by George Fyler Townsend). London: George Routledge and Sons.

The story above illustrates a point but lacks richness since it is being used as a vehicle to deliver a simple message. Encoding information is only one function of stories and any story will always have information encoded in it. When we limit stories in a premeditated way to carrying one or two simple messages, we throw away the opportunity for complexity to emerge. Although it is probably one of the most familiar functions of stories, it is often the least useful one for creating compelling experiential dialogues that can catapult learners to new insights. Experiential learning requires us to help people suspend their habitual ways of thinking to make room for new perspectives.

The most important function of stories is that they require active listening. By their nature, stories trick us into hearing ourselves and each other in deeper and fuller ways. When we listen actively to one another, we enter the world of another person. Our understanding of another person's story is gained by working with bits and pieces of our own stories to find common connections between the story being shared and our own experiences. While we are dependent on our experiences to construct meaning out of what another person shares with us, we are less likely to narrowly fixate on evaluating the story in terms of our world view. Like dreams that can present contradictory elements yet still be real (e.g., swimming and flying at the same time, or how a person who appears in a dream can be two people at the same time), stories invite us to work with conflicting things. When we actively listen to someone's story, we are not as emotionally invested in our points of view. Differences become opportunities. Empathy can be a wonderful byproduct of stories. Since experiential learning bridges the gap between people's current knowledge and desired learning, stories facilitate leaps of imagination that might never be realized by other modes of instruction.

Stories are wonderful tools for thinking. You can place people vicariously into a story and use it to work through new ideas and solutions. For example, if you were leading a discussion on leadership you might ask the group to explore how the story and characters of the *Wizard of Oz* offer insights into the nature of leadership. As long as people know the story, they will jump right into it and use it as a template for abstract thinking. The energy this creates in a group is contagious. The story mode of discussion will touch every kind of thinking and communication style in the room. Creative types will love coming up with zany connections between the *Wizard of Oz* and leadership, while more analytical types of people will enjoy exploring the details and nuances of the connections being found.

Stories as weapons or tools for healing are the last two functions of stories. When someone uses a story to coerce a point of view or manipulate people's perceptions to serve an agenda, it becomes dangerous. Influence is a natural and ever-present facet of communicating, but when the power of stories is used to maliciously mislead people it constitutes an abuse.

Whether we use stories as a weapon consciously or not, it's a violation of people's imagination and disrespects the space of active listening created by stories. Here's an example. I was attending a coastal planning meeting. During the course of heated debate on where boundaries of a no-fishing zone should be drawn, someone held up a picture of a handicapped person fishing off a pier that was located in an area of the no-fishing zone being proposed. A picture is worth a thousand words and a story is worth a thousand pictures. Put the two together and you have a powerful punch. The commissioners at the meeting were taken by the picture and its story about providing access for handicapped people to fish. It affected their votes. The pier depicted in the picture was not included in the commission's no-fishing zone. Later it was discovered that the picture had been posed; the person in the picture was not even handicapped. The picture and its story had been used as a weapon.

Conversely, stories can be used for healing. There is a rich tradition of the role of narrative in many therapeutic practices. Facilitating group processes even in an organizational setting can unearth some intense emotions and perceptions. Revisiting a story and examining how the story relates to other experiences adds unpredictable layers of meaning and dimensionality. During the process of sharing a story, dialoging with others about it, and reflecting, the story is released from the past and given meaning in the present. In this way stories provide the raw material for encouraging new insights that can lead to creative solutions and the possibility of healing.

When stories commingle with each other, pathways emerge. Stories can unlock novel ways of seeing ourselves and making sense of the world. I was facilitating a leadership workshop where, after sharing many experiences, a senior level executive became aware of a habit he had of showing disrespect toward his colleagues. Without any sermonizing or prescription on my part or by the group, this executive saw a pattern in his stories. These stories projected a reality he was not satisfied with and one that he wished to alter. Through the stories, he gained an invaluable lens that helped him to see himself more honestly and that gave him the courage to free himself from repeating self-defeating stories.

As you become more aware of how the nine functions of stories operate, you will get better at naturally leveraging their unique effects to facilitate breakthrough communication and learning. I no longer think about it. Sharing stories and eliciting people's stories is what I do every time I am leading a conversation with a group. I have developed sensitivity to how these functions of stories and their unique effects impact group processes. I strive to seize the opportunities they create while remaining attentive to the ethical implications of putting people in learning situations they may not want to be in. Stories can be raw, and not everyone wants to either look at him- or herself or be exposed in front of others. There are no hard-and-fast rules about this stuff. As you develop a feel for healthy boundaries, learn to watch people in the group carefully to discern subtle cues as to how much they are willing to share and how deeply they want to reflect on it with the group.

Stories Operate on Five Levels

For the sake of simplicity, we can envision stories operating on five basic levels. Each layer is built upon the previous one. Figure 1.2 depicts these levels as an iceberg. Telling stories is what we encounter on the surface. At the bottom of the iceberg, stories impact how we interact with the world. Our images of ourselves and our templates for how we react to people and situations is encrypted in our stories. The five levels are explained on the next page.

Techniques for Working with Stories   **11**

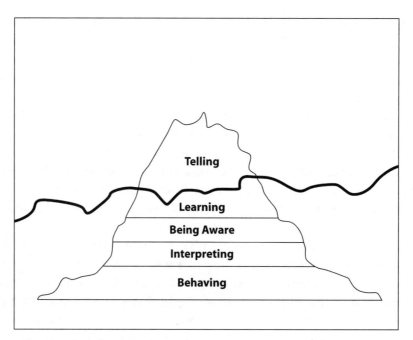

Figure 1.2. The Five Levels of Stories

1. Telling

We share our stories as a principal way of communicating. When someone tells us a story, we usually respond with a story of our own, and even if we don't, we recall one in our minds in order to understand what that person is saying. Having many stories to tell makes us versatile communicators.

2. Learning

We use stories to transmit learning. If a picture is worth a thousand words, a story is worth a thousand pictures. Complex and intricate thoughts and ideas can be elegantly woven in stories. Stories map to one another. We create relationships between stories and look for parallels between them. In this way, stories are also building blocks for learning. We learn by associating new pieces of information with existing ones. When experience remains isolated in a single domain, it is horribly inefficient. Roger Schank (founder of the Institute for the Learning Sciences at Northwestern University and founder of Socratic Arts) asserts that intelligence is the ability to easily index our vast array of experiences and make connections between old ones and new ones.

3. Being Aware

Since our experiences play a large role in forming who we are, stories are used to gain self-awareness. Our stories contain vital clues to who we are and how we view the world. We need to reflect on our experiences to get the most out of them.

Stories are like watching a videotape of our experiences. They give us access to our memories and provide a medium through which we can analyze the impact of these memories on our perceptions and identities.

4. Interpreting

We are constantly crafting stories to explain the world. However, it's important to realize that our interpretations are filtered through our perceptions, beliefs, attitudes, and biases.

The stories we craft are theories. We develop our "story theories" by combining our observations with perceptual filters. Our perceptual filters develop over time as a result of our experiences. And our experiences are accessible to us through memories that are archived as stories in our minds.

5. Behaving

We use stories to explain other people's behavior and develop strategies for how to interact with them. We are also capable of considering alternative behaviors that go against our ingrained ones by being aware of what stories describe our nature and by imagining alternative ones.

Stories are the templates upon which new behaviors can be projected and actualized. We use stories to gain an understanding of who we are. Collectively, our stories paint an accurate picture of who we are. If we can access this information, we give ourselves freedom. We do not need to react to the world. Becoming aware of what stories are influencing us enables us to be proactive versus reactive. In other words, we can break out of an old story and temporarily adopt a new one. I use the word "temporarily" because some behaviors may be more ingrained in us than others. Under certain circumstances, we may choose to bypass our reactions. On the other hand, there are other situations in which even a greater awareness of our stories will not alter our default behavior all the time.

Nine Ground Rules for Working with Stories

To be effective at working with stories in learning environments, there are nine ground rules to follow:

1. Be Able to Expand or Collapse a Story

Stories can vary in length. Stories can be as short as a sentence or two. In fact I have been in situations in which a single word becomes associated with a story already known by the group or that has emerged from my time with them. For example, consider the sentence, "The emperor has no clothes." If a group of learners were wrestling with a theme of mass denial, the reference to the classic Hans Christian Andersen story of an emperor who is wearing no clothes, and the reluctance of people to point this out, could bring quick clarity to learners.

As a facilitator, it is your job to decide what the right amount of detail for a story is. If you are using a story as an energizer or to give the group a chance to catch its breath, lavishing a story with rich detail may be a wonderful way of massaging people's tired brains and emotions. On the other hand, if you are stringing together a complex set of interconnections between ideas in a discussion and key learnings, your story will be more succinct. The composition of the group also factors into your decision of how much detail to include. This necessitates that you can reconstitute a story with either less or more detail, depending on your analysis of the group and its needs.

Even if you are not the one telling a story, it is your job as a facilitator to guide participants to share their stories with the appropriate amount of detail. This is done by acting as a good model, anticipating the tendencies of individuals, and, if necessary, giving them some constraints before they launch into their telling.

2. Incorporate Material Relevant to the Group into Stories

Good storytellers know how to customize a story to a group. Think back to when you were a kid and your teacher personalized a story by using your name or one of your favorite stuffed animals as a detail in the story. Didn't you feel engaged and excited to become an integral part of the story? Was your imagination stimulated? The same is true for adult learners. We love to see ourselves in the situations being painted by a compelling story. Our techniques for incorporating relevant material into stories with adult learners can be as simple as weaving in a personal fact to richer ones such as referencing other people's personal stories. As you become more adept at this, you will find yourself naturally weaving in all sorts of artifacts from the group's process or history. In this way, stories cease to be stale, since they offer tellers a way to stay invigorated. The very act of weaving in new material with the story will create opportunities for the teller to uncover new nooks and crannies of meaning.

3. Be Willing to Be Vulnerable with a Group

Stories are not for the faint of heart. Stories open the space between us and others. They are a sacred tool for deeper reflection and insight. We have to let go of our need to control the thoughts, reflections, and learning processes of others. In their truest sense, stories are not a behavioral tool for hitting the right button in others to produce a desired, predictable outcome. The experiential nature of story demands vulnerability. Are we willing to learn in front of others? Can we remove the artificial boundaries that we erect in learning environments to protect our authority? Stories broaden our awareness before they focus it. Imagine an hour glass. The top of the glass is wide. The sand drops down through a narrow crack before it falls into a wide basin below. Stories are similar in this respect. As we explore the interconnections between our stories and their relationship to other people's experiences, the learning environment might feel scattered and chaotic. People might ask, "Where is this going?" Inevitably, you will ask yourself the same question. Until suddenly the story drops through the narrow hole of analytical discourse and opens into a new vista of insight and meaning. The story has been a catalyst for learning and is a new buoy for anchoring future ones. None of this is possible if we do not make ourselves vulnerable with a group. Sharing a personal story is a wonderful way of softening a group and modeling the openness stories require to work their magic.

4. Be Authentic

Whether we are conscious of doing it or not, we are constantly evaluating the authenticity of others. Whenever we detect even a hint of falseness or any other form of selfishness or negative intentions in someone, we shut him or her out. Any hope of building a bridge constructed with mutual active listening is completely destroyed, and most of the time there is very little chance of rebuilding it once we lose the trust of others. You might share an experience or two as a means of engendering credibility with a group. However, avoid telling stories for self-aggrandizement. It never achieves the kind of long-lasting impacts of reflective, experiential learning that stories are perfectly suited for.

5. Make Sure There Is Congruence Between Your Stories and Your Behavior

We lessen the potential of our personal stories when our actions and stories do not correspond with each other. No one is asking you to be perfect. When leading a group, we often need to accentuate ideals. If there is a blatant contradiction between stories we tell and how we act, we will ruin the climate of trust, openness, and reflection we have created by working with stories.

6. Elicit More Stories Than You Tell

The shortest distance between two people is a story. One of the chief reasons to tell a story is to elicit them. Stories act as triggers. We want to draw stories out of people. As the number of personal experiences shared increases, so do the quality and quantity of experiential learning. Even if someone does not share his or her story out loud, your story will set off a series of internal reflective events. People scan their indexes of personal experiences to find ones that match or resonate with the ones we tell them. It is not always a direct one-to-one correspondence. In other words, the stories we elicit in others will not always have an easy-to-see relationship to our own. We are after connections.

Tip Box: Eliciting Stories

In order to elicit stories in others, we need to work on three levels:

Level	Name	Description
Level 1	Trust	• Building history with others • Creating joint stories • Having shared experiences
Level 2	Climate of Sharing	• Willingness to share our own experiences and be vulnerable • Inviting others to share • Demonstrate resonance and understanding of others' experiences • Pacing
Level 3	Attending	• Rephrasing questions • Developing alternative questions • Matching others' language

7. Be Open, Respectful, and Non-Judgmental of the Stories People Share

Treat all stories with respect. When someone shares a story, he or she has given us a part of him- or herself. Handle it accordingly. The fragile pieces of our identity rest in our narratives. Never feel entitled to know anyone's story. People will share what they want, when they are ready, and in a manner that does not violate their sense of themselves. However, you will be surprised at how willing and eager people are to exit the precarious myth of their separateness and embrace a sense of belonging granted by tying their experiences to those of others in a tapestry of shared consciousness.

The most vivid pictures we own are the stories in our hearts. Stories support a lattice of human experience. Each new story acts as a tendril tying us to the past, making the present significant, and giving shape to the future. Stories by their nature are a microcosm of who and how we are, so be sure you're always respectful and non-judgmental. We can never fully understand the mysteries of someone else's journey. Stories have no need to compete with one another, and stories exist to coexist with each other. Act as an unbiased, self-aware, gracious curator, and stories will usher in a cornucopia of delights and wisdom.

8. Connect Stories to One Another

Treat each story as a building block that can be pieced together with another one to generate greater understanding. Stories left in isolation are like cold statues in abandoned temples erected as grand testimonies of heroic accomplishments but devoid of depth and significance. I developed a group facilitation technique called Story Collaging™ (described in Part Two of this book) for helping groups see the connections between stories. Leave no stone unturned. As members of a group create a shared history, lots and lots of stories will naturally emerge. Your job is to remember these stories and constantly look for how they relate to one another. You are also tasked with encouraging others in the group to do the same thing.

Stories are reflection in motion. One story leads to another, and before you know it you have a mosaic of experiences crisscrossing with one another. Stories are like the tiny pieces of glass in a stained glass window. Every time the sun shines through, new colors and shades of meaning emerge. Story listeners function like the sun in our image of a stained glass window. This is one of the most exciting things I do as a facilitator. I never know what will surface. The stronger the connections between the stories and the greater the number of connections between them directly correlates with the quality of learning.

9. Build in More Room for Story Sharing When Designing Learning

Time to retire heavily scripted courses. Facilitating experiential learning with stories is not for the faint of heart. It requires guts, courage, authenticity, and an ability to think on your feet. Here's the secret: once you become accustomed to being in less control and collaborating with a group, the richer and more significant the learning will be. We must be willing to surrender a certain amount of our positional power to be effective. Chuck Hodell, in his book, *ISD from the Ground Up,* makes this point in a subtle way by saying, "The better the course goes, the less chance there is that anyone will appreciate the effort that went into it" (2000, p. 185). If you make stories a core part of your experiential learning strategy during an event though, you will be wiped out. As we discussed earlier in the chapter, stories require active listening, and this make them exhausting as well as exhilarating. Stories are the most effective when used as a tool to facilitate participant collaboration.

Even very technical topics or regulatory forms of learning can benefit from building in time for knowledge sharing through stories. Of course, topics that are softer in nature require lots of time and space for stories. As we have become more and more harried in our daily lives, we have lost the art of conversation. Good conversations are full of stories. When we design learning, less will always be more. I use other forms of instruction to give people variety and a break from the intense, reflective nature of dialogue through stories. Group dialogue saturated with stories needs to be at the heart of experiential learning. Even when we create event-driven experiences for people in learning, we are in essence giving them new stories to reflect on. In this way stories are effective because they help us enact our intentions and thoughts, rather than announce them. More traditional forms of instructional design are focused on instructing and telling us what we need to know. Stories always lead by offering examples and an endless playground for our imaginations to unearth new treasures.

As a general guideline, if you have not developed the course and there is very little room in the material for deviations or discussion, spend a few minutes at the beginning of the day of a multi-day session, after breaks, at the end of a learning module, or any place in which debriefings or questions have been built into the course to share and elicit stories from the group. When facilitating other people's course materials, I have been known to give people a break from didactic lecturing by giving folks some quiet time to digest the material on their own. This is followed by a quick recapitulation and an opportunity for people to ask questions. This usually gives me a few minutes to query the group for experiences and stories relevant to the material just read. Admittedly, some courses will not lend themselves to the use of stories. Or they may require you as facilitator to pinpoint spots in the courses and fine-tune the stories you tell. Remember that if you tell a story and there is not enough time for people to respond with their stories, whatever story you tell will be best served by a selfless attitude. Your story should not be about impressing others or driving a simple point home. Your story needs to be rich enough that it is evoking people's experiences. Ideally, you want to be able to process this with folks, but if there is not enough time just be sure your story is rich enough to cause people to reflect and synthesize their experiences in new ways.

Chapter Summary and Key Points

Stories play a central role in facilitating any kind of experiential learning, especially learning aimed at strengthening our communication skills. Developing breakthrough communication skills in ourselves and others requires a command of the nine functions of stories. These are the building blocks for simplifying the exchange of complex information and connecting with others. We concluded the chapter by discussing nine ground rules for working with stories. In the next chapter, we will identify nine story-based communication competencies that are critical for communication and use a tool to assess your command of them.

Key Points

Stories Function in Nine Ways

1. Empower a speaker

2. Create an environment

3. Bind and bond individuals

4. Engage our minds in active listening

5. Negotiate difference

6. Encode information

7. Tools for thinking

8. Serve as weapons

9. Bring about healing

Active listening is the most important aspect of stories and it is essential to breakthrough communication skills.

Stories offer a wealth of opportunities for eliciting insights.

Stories Operate on Five Levels

1. Telling

2. Learning

3. Being aware

4. Interpreting

5. Behaving

Nine Ground Rules for Working with Stories

1. Be able to expand or collapse a story.

2. Incorporate material relevant to the group into stories.

3. Be willing to be vulnerable with a group.

4. Be authentic.

5. Make sure there is congruence between your stories and your behavior.

6. Elicit more stories than you tell.

7. Be open, respectful, and non-judgmental of the stories people share.

8. Connect stories to one another.

9. Build in more room for story sharing when designing learning.

Techniques for Working with Stories   **19**

2

A Tool for Assessing Story-Based Communication Competencies

In this chapter we transition from the discussion of techniques of how to work with stories from the previous chapter to a tool for assessing your story-based communication competencies. Stories in communication work in subtle ways. After conducting some research with Fortune 500 leaders, I developed a competency model that consists of three rings and nine competencies (see Sharpe, 2005). The first part of the chapter explains the model and its relevance to developing breakthrough communication skills in yourself and others. The second part of the chapter is a self-assessment tool for measuring your mastery of the nine story-based communication competencies (SCCT). Depending on your preference, you may either go straight to the second part of the chapter and use the self-assessment tool or you may read about the model first.

Nine Story-Based Communication Competencies

The more I worked with stories, the more I realized there must be some essential competencies to being an effective communicator, learner, and thinker with stories. As I pored over piles of surveys and reviewed hours and hours of interviews, I began to notice clear repeating patterns. One of the things that struck me immediately was the central role stories play in communication. Yet despite the fact that they are so pervasive, we are not aware, purposeful, or strategic in how we use them. Although stories may be an obvious facet of communication, they're not something we seek to understand or leverage more effectively.

Figure 2.1 illustrates the competency model I developed from all the data collected. The model consists of three rings and nine competencies, which are further described in Table 2.1.

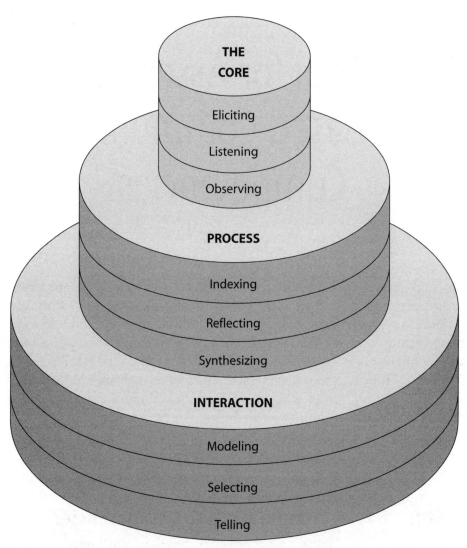

Figure 2.1. Story-Based Communication Competency Model

From Terrence L. Gargiulo, The *Strategic Use of Stories in Organizational Communication and Learning* (Armonk, NY: M.E. Sharpe, 2005). Copyright © by M.E. Sharpe, Inc. Used by permission.

Table 2.1. Description of Story-Based Communication Competency Model

Ring	Competency	Description
Interaction *Describes how we use stories to connect with others and communicate.*	Modeling	Being aware of one's actions and using them to create lasting impressions in the eyes of others. Employing a variety of analogical techniques to bring an idea or concept alive.
	Telling	Relaying a story with authenticity that paints a vivid, engaging picture for listeners.
	Selecting	Picking a story that is appropriate to the situation at hand and that clearly communicates concepts, ideas, or feelings.
Process *Describes how we work with experiences to transform them into meaningful and reusable stories.*	Indexing	Developing a flexible, vast, mental schema for retrieval of experiences and knowledge.
	Synthesizing	Finding patterns in new experiences and creating connections between them and old ones.
	Reflecting	Reviewing experiences with circumspection and extracting knowledge from them.
The Core *Describes how we open ourselves to be aware of and sensitive to stories.*	Eliciting	Asking questions and finding ways to pull stories from others.
	Listening	Absorbing stories and invoking the imagination to enter them in a fundamental and deep way.
	Observing	Practicing mindfulness to become aware of the stories implicit in others' words and actions.

From Terrence L. Gargiulo, The *Strategic Use of Stories in Organizational Communication and Learning* (Armonk, NY: M.E. Sharpe, 2005). Copyright © by M.E. Sharpe, Inc. Used by permission.

Interaction Ring

The rings represent three levels of personal story competencies related to communicating and learning. Each ring consists of three competencies. The outermost ring of Interaction characterizes the competencies we use to engage with the external world. Many people mistakenly assume that using stories well requires little besides knowing what stories to select and being good at telling them. Although these are useful competencies, they are superficial compared to the others. The interaction ring also houses the modeling competency.

There are two levels to the competency of modeling. The first level describes how our actions model our beliefs, attitudes, and values. Through our actions we create stories. People are far more likely to remember our actions than our words. Whether they do it consciously or unconsciously, people observe our actions and look for incongruence between our words and behaviors. We have the ability to create stories by being mindful of how our actions impact the people around us. Memorable actions become part of other people's stories. Furthermore, our actions have the potential to cause others to reflect. The second level to the modeling competency is our ability to create compelling representations of the concepts we try to communicate to others. Developing a facility with analogies, metaphors, word pictures, and visuals is a subcomponent of this competency.

Process Ring

The second ring of the map is the Process ring. It is characterized by all of the internal things that we do in our minds when we are conscious of our stories and the stories around us. It is hard to discuss the three competencies in this ring in any causal order because these internal processes of indexing, synthesizing, and reflecting happen most of the time in parallel. The reflection competency is the discipline we develop in stopping to notice our stories. To paraphrase a Greek philosopher, "an unexamined story is not worth having." Reflection can be broken down into four parts:

1. Reflection—the manner in which we use stories to visualize and relive our experiences.
2. Sitting—being still to linger in our experiences.
3. Inviting—involves actively looking for new insights.
4. Sifting—the review and analysis of the insights that emerge.

While we gather new insights from our own stories, a highly developed capacity for reflection also makes us more mindful of others and their thoughts, feeling, and experiences. We are less likely to react to people. Reflection gives us a chance to behave proactively and continually revise our perceptual filters.

The second competency in the Process ring is synthesizing. By reflecting on our stories, we begin to find connections with other stories and other domains of knowledge. Through synthesis we discover relationships between previously unrelated experiences, ideas, concepts, and knowledge. We take the new pieces of information and transform them into insights. The link between learning and stories is found in this competency. Being effective at doing this requires all three competencies of reflecting, synthesizing, and indexing.

The last competency in the Process ring is indexing. Our experiences recorded as stories in our memories do not fit into neat categories. Every experience can be indexed, re-indexed, and cross-indexed in a variety of ways. This is further complicated by the fact that each of us develops his or her own indexing schemes. You and I will not use the same keys to codify our experiences and the learning or knowledge that result from them. Developing a rich index enables us to quickly see the applicability of our stories in different situations. We can uncover patterns of relevance and encounter greater resonance between others' experiences and our own by deliberately maintaining a diverse index.

Core Ring

The third ring of the map is the Core. It contains the central competencies that are at the heart of using stories effectively to be a better communicator and learner. All the competencies found in the other rings build off of the central ones of eliciting, listening, and observing. Listening is the common thread to the three competencies found in the Core; for example, being able to elicit stories demands sensitivity and attentiveness to the stories around oneself. Drawing stories out of others requires astute observation skills.

The observation competency is broken down into five parts:

1. Care/Intention—cultivating genuine interest in others.
2. Self-Awareness—examining impressions observed, assumptions made, conclusions drawn, and behaviors.
3. Sensitivity—increasing our attention to external stimuli.
4. External Focus—shifting and purposefully directing the focus of our attention.
5. Process Dialogue—tracking how perceptions are being formed.

We discover what questions to ask or what stories to tell in order to stimulate the storytelling of others by watching for cues in their words and actions. We must also be equally aware of our own thought processes. Listening ties them all together and involves more than hearing. As we gather information, listening engages our imaginations. What we hear is fused with our experiences. The new information comingles with the old to become relevant and immediate; otherwise, it is dead on arrival. We can communicate more by eliciting stories than by telling them. Consequently, a greater value is given to the competencies found in the Core than to those in the Interaction ring of the model. Later in this chapter when you use the self-assessment tool, you will see that this weighting of competencies in the Core is built into the tool.

These nine competencies represent the communication and learning competencies one needs to develop in order to be an effective facilitator of experiential learning with stories. For more ideas on how to develop these competencies, see *The Strategic Use of Stories in Organizational Communication Learning*. The whole last section of the book has a collection of self-development exercises for developing these competencies, which go beyond the facilitator. From my experience, group members who have well-developed story competencies are very effective communicators, learners, and thinkers.

Story-Based Communication Competency Self-Assessment Tool (SCCT)

With the help of Professor David Boje at New Mexico State University, co-founder of the Storytelling Organization Institute (STORI Institute), and graduate student Michele Auzene, we developed a tool for measuring the nine story-based communication competencies. This is a validated instrument. Additional data is being collected to understand how this tool relates to other highly regarded and widely used tools such as the *Leadership Practices Inventory* by Kouzes and Posner and the Myers-Briggs Personality Type Indicator™. The tool is introduced in this book as a self-assessment; however, other coaching and 360-degree feedback versions are also available. It will give you wonderful insights into your strengths as a communicator and help you see a picture of how all the competencies must work in concert in order to ensure great communication.

Instructions

Respond to the eighty questions in this tool using the following rating scale:

7 = Almost Always	6 = Very Frequently	5 = Usually	4 = Sometimes	3 = Once in a While	2 = Rarely	1 = Almost Never

Consider each statement independently. If you are assessing your skills within a specific context (e.g., your work environment versus your home environment), be sure to consider each statement within that context. Consider the frequency with which *you normally engage in the stated activity or behavior*. The more accurately you respond to each statement, the better your overall score will reflect your actual story-based communication competencies.

Once you have completed the assessment, transfer your responses to the scoring table and follow the scoring instructions found there.

SCCT is reprinted with permission from MAKINGSTORIES.net. Copies of the instrument and supporting materials can be obtained from www.makingstories.net.

Here are some tips to help you complete and gain the most value from the assessment:

1. Consider the full range of responses. A score of "4" represents dead center, so this is a useful starting point. From there, consider the three possible scores to each side as "high, "medium," and "low" frequency within the upper and lower range. Reserve a score of 7 for those statements that are highly reflective of your behavior and that you engage in almost automatically. Likewise, reserve a score of 1 for those statements that truly seem outside of your normal situational response.

2. Be mindful of the context of the assessment. We sometimes engage in different behaviors in our personal and professional lives. If you are assessing yourself in a particular context, say at work, imagine yourself in that environment on a typical day, and respond accordingly.

3. Complete the assessment in a single sitting. Stopping and starting might result in inconsistent use of the scoring range.

4. Use the results of the assessment as an indicator of your strength in each of the three competency rings of the Competency Model (Core, Processing, Interaction). By studying the individual scores of all nine competencies that comprise the model, you can determine specific storytelling skills that you may wish to improve or maximize as key components of your communication and story-telling style.

SCCT is reprinted with permission from MAKINGSTORIES.net. Copies of the instrument and supporting materials can be obtained from www.makingstories.net.

7 = Almost   6 = Very   5 = Usually   4 = Sometimes   3 = Once   2 = Rarely   1 = Almost
   Always   Frequently   in a While   Never

The Self-Assessment Tool

_____ 1. I share my professional experiences with others.

_____ 2. I have a genuine interest in people.

_____ 3. I paraphrase what others are saying to confirm what they are communicating.

_____ 4. I think about what I've learned from my experiences.

_____ 5. I use visualization as a strategy for reflecting on my experiences.

_____ 6. I transform what I have learned from my experiences into wisdom.

_____ 7. I use my body language and gestures when I tell stories.

_____ 8. I adjust the length and details of my story to fit the situation.

_____ 9. I reflect on my experiences.

_____ 10. I share my personal experiences with others.

_____ 11. I care about the success of people around me.

_____ 12. I paraphrase what others are saying to validate what they are communicating.

_____ 13. I am aware of experiences that have influenced my values, beliefs, and attitudes.

_____ 14. I recall the sensory details of my experiences.

_____ 15. I am open to learning from other people's experiences.

_____ 16. I am willing to share my emotions with others.

_____ 17. I allow others to interject their thoughts and experiences during a conversation.

_____ 18. I have a large collection of stories.

_____ 19. I encourage others to share their personal experiences.

_____ 20. I have a strong sense of my strengths.

_____ 21. I ask clarifying questions.

_____ 22. I am aware of how my values, beliefs, and attitudes shape my understanding.

_____ 23. I relive the thoughts and emotions of my experiences.

SCCT is reprinted with permission from MAKINGSTORIES.net. Copies of the instrument and supporting materials can be obtained from www.makingstories.net.

7 = Almost   6 = Very   5 = Usually   4 = Sometimes   3 = Once   2 = Rarely   1 = Almost
    Always   Frequently   in a While   Never

_____ 24. I make sense of things by actively searching for and extracting knowledge from my previous experiences.

_____ 25. I create an environment in which other people share their emotions along with "facts" and "data."

_____ 26. I tell stories with a specific purpose in mind.

_____ 27. I can easily find relevant experiences to share.

_____ 28. I encourage others to share their professional experiences.

_____ 29. I have a strong sense of my weaknesses.

_____ 30. I probe others to validate my interpretation of what is being shared.

_____ 31. I share past experiences with others to help them understand my worldview.

_____ 32. I make a point to remember my interpersonal interactions with others.

_____ 33. I connect my insights from one realm of activity to another.

_____ 34. I create metaphors to help people connect with me or with the information that I am sharing.

_____ 35. I spontaneously share my experiences.

_____ 36. I share experiences that enrich conversations.

_____ 37. I seek to create a climate of sharing.

_____ 38. I have a strong sense of my accomplishments.

_____ 39. I ask follow-up questions to enhance my understanding.

_____ 40. I interpret situations as they are occurring.

_____ 41. I review my experiences without judging them.

_____ 42. I see interrelationships between my experiences.

_____ 43. I create analogies to help people connect with me or with the information that I am sharing.

_____ 44. I use metaphors when I communicate.

_____ 45. I can recall experiences that express who I am.

_____ 46. I am willing to be vulnerable with others.

_____ 47. My interactions with others are guided by a strong understanding of myself.

SCCT is reprinted with permission from MAKINGSTORIES.net. Copies of the instrument and supporting materials can be obtained from www.makingstories.net.

7 = Almost Always	6 = Very Frequently	5 = Usually	4 = Sometimes	3 = Once in a While	2 = Rarely	1 = Almost Never

_____ 48. I avoid judging the value, importance, or quality of another person's experience.

_____ 49. I am aware of how I interpret things I hear and see around me.

_____ 50. I treat each of my experiences with a fresh and open mind.

_____ 51. I review my experiences to help me make sense of current situations.

_____ 52. I use humor to help people connect with me or see things in new ways.

_____ 53. I use anecdotes when I communicate.

_____ 54. I can find experiences that speak to others.

_____ 55. I respect others' perspectives.

_____ 56. I pay attention to the feelings of others.

_____ 57. I see situations and experiences from the eyes of others.

_____ 58. I look at my experiences from multiple perspectives.

_____ 59. I search my experiences to look for new and different possibilities.

_____ 60. I make room for back-and-forth conversation to generate new ideas and thinking.

_____ 61. I use questions when I communicate.

_____ 62. I seek to understand others' perspectives.

_____ 63. I am sensitive to the energy, thoughts, and moods of others.

_____ 64. I have a database of experiences that allows me to connect past and present experiences.

_____ 65. I am open to learning from my previous experiences in new and different ways.

_____ 66. I query my experiences to shape new meaning.

_____ 67. I acknowledge others for the contributions they make.

_____ 68. I vary the volume and tone of my voice when I communicate.

_____ 69. I rephrase and ask multiple questions to help others recall their experiences.

_____ 70. I purposefully review my interactions with others.

_____ 71. I review my experiences to learn from them.

_____ 72. I validate others' experiences.

SCCT is reprinted with permission from MAKINGSTORIES.net. Copies of the instrument and supporting materials can be obtained from www.makingstories.net.

7 = Almost   6 = Very   5 = Usually   4 = Sometimes   3 = Once   2 = Rarely   1 = Almost
   Always   Frequently   in a While   Never

_____ 73. I maintain eye contact when I communicate.

_____ 74. I adjust my speech to match the style of others when helping them recall their experiences.

_____ 75. I am aware of how I filter my experiences through my values, beliefs, and attitudes.

_____ 76. I understand my experiences in many ways, resulting in a rich variety of insights.

_____ 77. I am skilled at drawing stories from others.

_____ 78. I make choices about my behavior using insights from previous experience.

_____ 79. I invite my listeners to add details, contribute comments, and anticipate the direction the conversation.

_____ 80. I share my experiences in ways that encourage others to be open with me.

Transfer your responses to each of the eighty statements in the SCCT to the Scoring Table. Statements are listed from left to right in numeric order to help you with this process. Once you have transferred your responses, total the scores in each of the six columns, which correspond to the six storytelling competencies that comprise the three rings of the Competency Model. The columns are coded as follows:

Core Competencies	**Processing Competencies**	**Interaction Competencies**
Eliciting (C-ELI)	Indexing (P-IND)	Modeling (I-MOD)
Observing (C-OBS)	Reflecting (P-REF)	Telling (I-MOD)
Listening (C-LIS)	Synthesizing (P-SYN)	Selecting (I-SEL)

Total the three columns for each of the competency rings (Core, Processing, Interaction) and record them in the next row of the table. Finally, using the divisor indicated for each individual competency and for the complete competency ring, calculate your final scores. Convert the result to a percentage by moving the decimal point two places to the right, rounding off the third decimal place. This will give you a score indicating the frequency with which you normally engage in activities and behaviors associated with each individual competency and with each of the three competency rings as a whole.

SCCT is reprinted with permission from MAKINGSTORIES.net. Copies of the instrument and supporting materials can be obtained from www.makingstories.net.

Here's an example:

If you scored 55 in the C-ELI column, 47 in the C-OBS column, and 38 in the C-LIS column, your scores would look like this:

Eliciting (C-ELI): 55 divided by 84 = 0.654 = **65 percent**

Observing (C-OBS): 47 divided by 70 = 0.671 = **67 percent**

Listening (C-LIS): 38 divided by 49 = 0.775 = **78 percent**

Total Core Competencies Score: 55+47+38 = 140 divided by 203 = 0.689 = **69 percent**

These scores would indicate that you engage in Core competency behaviors 69 percent of the time within the context of the situation being assessed. Your strongest skills are in the Listening competency, where you engage associated activities and behaviors 78 percent of the time. Your skills in the Eliciting and Observing competencies are a bit lower at 65 percent and 67 percent, respectively.

Scoring Table

C-ELI	C-OBS	C-LIS	P-IND	P-REF	P-SYN	I-MOD	I-TEL	I-SEL
1.	2.	3.	4	5.	6.	7.	8.	9.
10.	11.	12.	13.	14.	15.	16.	17.	18.
19.	20.	21.	22.	23.	24.	25.	26.	27.
28.	29.	30.	31.	32.	33.	34.	35.	36.
37.	38.	39.	40.	41.	42.	43.	44.	45.
46.	47.	48.	49.	50.	51.	52.	53.	54.
55.	56.	57.	X	58.	59.	60.	61.	X
62.	63.	X	64.	65.	66.	67.	68.	X
69.	70.	X	X	71.	X	72.	73.	
74.	75.	X		76.			X	
77.				78.			79.	
80.								
n=	n=	n=	N=	n=	n=	n=	n=	n=
C-ELI	C-OBS	C-LIS	P-IND	P-REF	P-SYN	I-MOD	I-TEL	I-SEL
n/84:	n/70:	n/49:	n/49:	n/77:	n/56:	n/63:	n/70:	n/42:
Core			Processing			Interaction		
(n____/203):			(n____/196):			(n____/175):		

Comprehensive Competency Score

Using the *point totals* (not the percentage calculations) from the nine individual competency columns, calculate the following:

CORE Competency Total Points = _____

PROCESSING Competency Total Points = _____

INTERACTION Competency Total Points = _____

TOTAL POINTS = _____ divided by 560 = _____.

Convert to a percentage (move the decimal point two places to the right) for your final score of _____.

Story-Based Communication Competency Tool Scoring Graph

By graphing your competency scores here, you can create a visual representation of your storytelling skills. Use the first three bars for each competency ring to graph individual competency scores. In the fourth bar for each competency ring, enter your overall score for that ring. In the final bar, labeled "Overall," enter your comprehensive score.

SCORING GRAPH

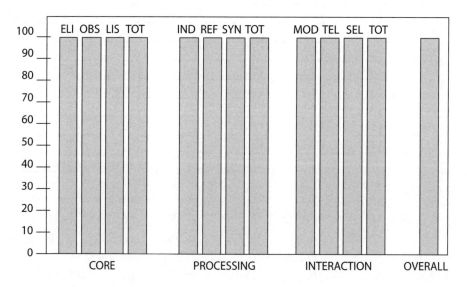

SCCT is reprinted with permission from MAKINGSTORIES.net. Copies of the instrument and supporting materials can be obtained from www.makingstories.net.

Applying the Results

Let's return to our example scoring of Core competencies. In our example, the final scores looked like this:

Eliciting (C-ELI): 55 divided by 84 = 0.654 = **65 percent**

Observing (C-OBS): 47 divided by 70 = 0.671 = **67 percent**

Listening (C-LIS): 38 divided by 49 = 0.775 = **78 percent**

Total Core Competencies Score: 55+47+38 = 140 divided by 203 = 0.689 = **69 percent**

We observed that these scores indicate that you engage in Core competency behaviors 69 percent of the time within the context of the situation being assessed. Your strongest skills are in the Listening competency, where you engage associated activities and behaviors 78 percent of the time. Your skills in the Eliciting and Observing competencies are a bit lower at 65 percent and 67 percent, respectively. What does this mean? And how can you use these results to understand and improve your storytelling skills?

First, it's important that you continue practicing good listening skills. Good listening skills are at the heart of effective storytelling, and effective storytelling leads to communication breakthroughs, and you have rated yourself as 78 percent effective in this area. While there is room for improvement, you are fairly competent in this area. Further improvement is largely a matter of consciously and deliberately engaging these behaviors more frequently until they become further ingrained in your skills set.

Because the Core competencies are so well integrated, focused attention toward improving your listening skills will automatically lead to improvements in the Eliciting and Observing competencies. However, your skills in these areas are significantly lower, and you should also work to improve these through direct practice. Practice mindfulness as you engage the competencies and notice the impact your behavior has on others. You might want to keep a notebook throughout this process, noting those behaviors and activities that are most helpful to you. Remember, we all have unique styles of communicating, and you will need to assess how different approaches and techniques work for you.

Follow a similar process in applying the results from each competency ring of the model, being sure to consider each of the three competencies within a ring in relation to the other two. It might be helpful to focus on one competency ring at a time as you work to improve your skills. You will, however, quickly realize that

SCCT is reprinted with permission from MAKINGSTORIES.net. Copies of the instrument and supporting materials can be obtained from www.makingstories.net.

improvement in any one of the nine competencies will lead to improvement in several others.

As with any tool, try not to become overly focused on labels or results. The assessment is meant to promote greater self-awareness and dialogue with your self and others to stretch and grow in new directions. There are low scores but there are no bad scores; and until every one of us uses all of these competencies 100 percent of the time, there is a lot of room for us to grow, even if our scores are high. After a period of practice, you should retake the SCCT. As before, respond to each statement as honestly as possible to ensure your final scores accurately reflect your actual skills level.

Copies of the SCCT tool, guide for facilitators, and self-development exercises for participants can be ordered from my website or you can use the order form on the CD-ROM.

SCCT is reprinted with permission from MAKINGSTORIES.net. Copies of the instrument and supporting materials can be obtained from www.makingstories.net.

Once Upon a Time

Chapter Summary and Key Points

Stories are so much a part of how we communicate that it's easy to take them for granted. There is a lot going on under the surface. We examined a story-based communication competency model derived from research with Fortune 500 companies that captures the subtleties of how stories work in communication. The model consists of nine competencies distributed in three rings. Our challenge is to put these nine competencies to work all the time in order to become the best communicator we can be. We then presented a tool for assessing these competencies. Chapter 3 will look at how we use stories to make sense of the world around us and communicate our understanding to others.

Key Points

The nine story-based communication competencies sit in three rings: Interaction, Process, and Core. The competencies are:

1. Selecting
2. Telling
3. Modeling
4. Indexing
5. Synthesizing
6. Reflecting
7. Eliciting
8. Listening
9. Observing

The most important competencies for developing breakthrough communication skills in yourself and others sit in the Core. Of these, the Listening competency is the most important.

The Story-Based Communication Competency Tool (SCCT) assesses the frequency with which one uses the nine competencies as a communicator. The SCCT helps us understand our unique mix of communication strengths and the interrelationship among them.

Developing breakthrough communication skills requires mastering the nine story-based communication competencies.

3

Sense Making and Stories

Up to this point, we have reviewed some techniques for how to use stories to develop breakthrough communication skills and examined nine essential communication competencies. We emphasized the importance of understanding our unique blend of competencies. The second part of the book will provide you with proven experiential activities that will help you develop these competencies in others. In this chapter we will look at how we rely on stories to make sense of the world around us. When we are leading a discussion, we should strive to elicit stories from others. This chapter prepares you for how to handle these stories. We will explore the concept of sense making with stories and outline four dynamics we need to be aware of when we work with people's stories. Our goal is to increase people's opportunities to discover new insights through their sense making work with stories.

Sense Making with Stories

Our job is to help people work with their stories to generate new meanings, learning, and insights. This is not as simple as it may appear. Stories operate on lots of different levels. Unless we become sensitized to the various ways people make sense of their stories, we will miss precious opportunities to help them find meaning that can guide their behaviors in new directions.

According to David Boje, professor of management at New Mexico State University, who has been studying stories and narrative for over thirty years, "sense making is more about *story-listening* than *story-telling*." I like to say that stories are the music we dance to. Stories are complex. The utterance of a story produces a vast array of subtle phenomena. Our hearts, minds, and bodies race in a myriad of ways. Sense making with stories engages our entire being. We embody our stories, and our stories are a concrete projection of who we are.

During a recent conference on storytelling and complexity sponsored by the STORI Institute, David discussed eight forms of sense making. For our purposes, the details of these eight forms of sense making are not critical. What is important is that, although these eight forms of sense making are happening in parallel, we cannot attend to all of them at the same time. This has a huge implication for us as facilitators. While we are processing a story using one of these forms of sense making, other people will be engaged in different ones. Humility and flexibility are keys to our effectiveness. Humble, because no matter how sharp and perceptive we may be, we cannot be aware of or process all the forms of sense making going on. Flexible, because we need to learn how to shift in and out of different forms of sense making and never become too entrenched in our interpretations.

Our responsibility as a facilitator is never to forget that there are multiple forms of sense making happening all the time. As we help a group untangle the threads of a story, we must accept that we will not be able to unpack all of a story's meaning. We are working with fragments. Some of these fragments of meaning will collide and clash with each other. During a phone interview with David, he offered me a wonderful analogy to explain this phenomenon of fragmentary sense making. He cited the classic story of the blind men and the elephant. In the story, blind men are given an opportunity to touch various body parts of an elephant in an effort to ascertain its identity. None of them has access to all the information, so if they never compare notes and synthesize their impressions they will never discover the elephant. Breaking apart experiences can turn them into meaningless pieces of unconnected information. Our sense making remains impotent and potentially dangerous when we base our actions on it.

Sense making with stories has the potential to facilitate "aha" moments for people. These are epiphanies that are a result of reflective space created by stories. Meanings bubble up from a well of possibilities. These insights emerge in the "here and now." As facilitators we can create environments saturated with stories and sense making. When we let go of directing the group or controlling its sense-making processes, people become witnesses to each other's stories. All the various forms of sense making with stories ferment with each other, creating a brew steeped in rich flavors.

This is a bit abstract, so let me provide an illustration of story sense making that is in the "here and now." As you read the story, think about how the emperor in the story makes sense of his experience.

Three Questions—by Leo Tolstoy

One day it occurred to a certain emperor that if he only knew the answers to three questions, he would never stray in any matter.

- What is the best time to do each thing?
- Who are the most important people to work with?
- What is the most important thing to do at all times?

The emperor issued a decree throughout his kingdom announcing that whoever could answer the questions would receive a great reward. Many who read the decree made their way to the palace at once, each person with a different answer.

In reply to the first question, one person advised that the emperor make up a thorough time schedule, consecrating every hour, day, month, and year for certain tasks and then follow the schedule to the letter. Only then could he hope to do every task at the right time.

Another person replied that it was impossible to plan in advance and that the emperor should put all vain amusements aside and remain attentive to everything in order to know what to do at what time.

Someone else insisted that, by himself, the emperor could never hope to have all the foresight and competence necessary to decide when to do each and every task and what he really needed was to set up a Council of the Wise and then to act according to their advice.

Someone else said that certain matters required immediate decisions and could not wait for consultation, but if he wanted to know in advance what was going to happen he should consult magicians and soothsayers.

The responses to the second question also lacked accord.

One person said that the emperor needed to place all his trust in administrators, another urged reliance on priests and monks, while others recommended physicians. Still others put their faith in warriors.

The third question drew a similar variety of answers. Some said science was the most important pursuit. Others insisted on religion. Yet others claimed the most important thing was military skill.

The emperor was not pleased with any of the answers, and no reward was given.

After several nights of reflection, the emperor resolved to visit a hermit who lived up on the mountain and was said to be an enlightened man. The emperor wished to find the hermit to ask him the three questions, although he knew the hermit never left the mountains and was known to receive only the poor, refusing to have anything to do with persons of wealth or power. So the emperor disguised himself as a simple peasant and ordered his attendants to wait for him at the foot of the mountain while he climbed the slope alone to seek the hermit.

Reaching the holy man's dwelling place, the emperor found the hermit digging a garden in front of his hut. When the hermit saw the stranger, he nodded his head in greeting and continued to dig. The labor was obviously hard on him. He was an old man, and each time he thrust his spade into the ground to turn the earth, he heaved heavily.

The emperor approached him and said, "I have come here to ask your help with three questions: When is the best time to do each thing? Who are the most important people to work with? What is the most important thing to do at all times?"

The hermit listened attentively, but only patted the emperor on the shoulder and continued digging. The emperor said, "You must be tired. Here, let me give you a hand with that." The hermit thanked him, handed the emperor the spade, and then sat down on the ground to rest.

After he had dug two rows, the emperor stopped and turned to the hermit and repeated his three questions. The hermit still did not answer, but instead stood up and pointed to the spade and said, "Why don't you rest now? I can take over again." But the emperor continued to dig. One hour passed, then two. Finally the sun began to set behind the mountain. The emperor put down the spade and said to the hermit, "I came here to ask if you could answer my three questions. But if you can't give me any answer, please let me know so that I can get on my way home."

The hermit lifted his head and asked the emperor, "Do you hear someone running over there?" The emperor turned his head. They both saw a man with a long white beard emerge from the woods. He ran wildly, pressing his hands against a bloody wound in his stomach. The man ran toward the emperor before falling unconscious to the ground, where he lay groaning. Opening the man's clothing, the emperor and hermit saw that the man had received a deep gash. The emperor cleaned the wound thoroughly and then used his own shirt to bandage it, but the blood completely soaked it within minutes. He rinsed the shirt out and bandaged the wound a second time and continued to do so until the flow of blood had stopped.

At last the wounded man regained consciousness and asked for a drink of water. The emperor ran down to the stream and brought back a

Once Upon a Time

jug of fresh water. Meanwhile, the sun had disappeared and the night air had begun to turn cold. The hermit gave the emperor a hand in carrying the man into the hut, where they laid him down on the hermit's bed. The man closed his eyes and lay quietly. The emperor was worn out from the long day of climbing the mountain and digging the garden. Leaning against the doorway, he fell asleep. When he rose, the sun had already risen over the mountain. For a moment he forgot where he was and what he had come here for. He looked over to the bed and saw the wounded man also looking around him in confusion. When he saw the emperor, he stared at him intently and then said in a faint whisper, "Please forgive me."

"But what have you done that I should forgive you?" the emperor asked.

"You do not know me, your majesty, but I know you. I was your sworn enemy, and I had vowed to take vengeance on you, for during the last war you killed my brother and seized my property. When I learned that you were coming alone to the mountain to meet the hermit, I resolved to surprise you on your way back to kill you. But after waiting a long time there was still no sign of you, and so I left my ambush in order to seek you out. But instead of finding you, I came across your attendants, who recognized me, giving me this wound. Luckily, I escaped and ran here. If I hadn't met you I would surely be dead by now. I had intended to kill you, but instead you saved my life! I am ashamed and grateful beyond words. If I live, I vow to be your servant for the rest of my life, and I will bid my children and grandchildren to do the same. Please grant me your forgiveness."

The emperor was overjoyed to see that he was so easily reconciled with a former enemy. He not only forgave the man but promised to return all the man's property and to send his own physician and servants to wait on the man until he was completely healed. After ordering his attendants to take the man home, the emperor returned to see the hermit. Before returning to the palace, the emperor wanted to repeat his three questions one last time. He found the hermit sowing seeds in the earth they had dug the day before.

The hermit stood up and looked at the emperor. "But your questions have already been answered."

"How's that?" the emperor asked, puzzled.

"Yesterday, if you had not taken pity on my age and given me a hand with digging these beds, you would have been attacked by that man on your way home. Then you would have deeply regretted not staying with me. Therefore, the most important time was the time you were digging in

Sense Making and Stories   **43**

the beds, the most important person was myself, and the most important pursuit was to help me. Later, when the wounded man ran up here, the most important time was the time you spent dressing his wound, for if you had not cared for him he would have died and you would have lost the chance to be reconciled with him. Likewise, he was the most important person, and the most important pursuit was taking care of his wound. Remember that there is only one important time and it is Now. The present moment is the only time over which we have dominion. The most important person is always the person with whom you are, who is right before you, for who knows if you will have dealings with any other person in the future. The most important pursuit is making that person, the one standing at your side, happy, for that alone is the pursuit of life."

Interpretation of Story and Its Relation to Sense Making

Tolstoy's story is a marvelous illustration of sense making. The emperor begins with three earnest questions. None of the answers he receives resonate with him, so he seeks the advice of a wise hermit. We can view the hermit as a facilitator. While we may lack the wisdom of the hermit, we operate as guides to people's questions.

On the surface it appears that the hermit tells the emperor what he has learned. Although the hermit is very direct in his remarks, he is acting more as catalyst than as a preacher. The hermit is nudging the emperor. This is a fine line we walk as facilitators, but I feel it is important to take these risks. We cannot be completely neutral or objective with how we are making sense of other people's stories. We form opinions and make assumptions. As a facilitator, I check my assumptions and adjust my tack based on the feedback I receive. When I have some confidence about what I am perceiving and interpreting, I test the waters.

Just as the hermit struggles under the distress of hard work of sowing his garden to reap its rewards, so must the emperor discover meaning in his experience by being present in the here and now. It's no coincidence that the hermit shares his work with the emperor. This forms a social contract. It demonstrates the emperor's willingness to seek answers to his questions and make sense of his stories. I love how the hermit creates a learning experience for the emperor out of nothing. The "moment" presents an opportunity to seek meaning. It is not an orchestrated, contrived, or controlled event. It happens.

The emperor embarks on a spontaneous adventure and participates in a new set of experiences. These experiences become his stories and opportunities for sense making. The emperor's new story is a container for multiple ones—each one with its own set of associations. For example, the emperor's sworn enemy has stories that form intersecting threads of life-changing significance for the two characters. The emperor is no longer an enemy and the emperor gains new emotional perspective on the impact of his past actions on others. All of these things are gifts that rise from the reflective, experiential meaning created in the moment.

Stories are saturated with potential. Networks of stories live within each other and create endless chains of meaning. The answers to the emperor's questions emerge as a result of a sense-making process that yields an epiphany. The hermit invites the emperor to reflect on his recent experience and see how it is a perfect backdrop to form answers to his questions. The meaning he discovers is what Professor David Boje terms as "emergent." The activities in this book are intended to help people use stories to experience as much of this kind of emergent sense making as possible.

Facilitator's Guide to Helping Others Make Sense of Their Stories

Helping others make sense of stories is one of the trickiest things we do as facilitators. As desirable as it might be, it is impossible to always be involved in sense making that is in the here and now. When I teach facilitation of stories, I highlight four dynamics to be mindful of when people are working with stories:

- Rationalization
- Extraction
- Projection
- Insight

In the next section I define and summarize each sense-making dynamic. After each description there is a list of benefits and pitfalls.

Four Dynamics of Working with Stories

1. Rationalizations. Stories are used to justify existing ideas, opinions, thoughts, emotions, or behaviors. Stories are not used to find new meanings, but rather to support and solidify existing personal or group theories and interpretations.

Benefits of Sense Making Through Rationalization
- Helpful in reinforcing insights gained from previous reflective activities.
- For a facilitator or listener, sense making of stories through rationalization provides quick insight to prevalent patterns of thought, behavior, defense mechanisms, and sources of resistance.

- Rationalizations can be used to pinpoint other experiences that correspond to and support the current interpretation being shared. If a person is having trouble recognizing that he is making sense of the current story by fitting it into a predefined mold of meaning, use probing questions to invite him to reconsider past experiences in a new light.

Pitfalls of Sense Making Through Rationalization
- Interpretations might be inaccurate or lead to self-fulfilling prophecies.
- Rationalizations can be abused as a way of controlling or limiting of sense making, especially when it's used to support arguments.

2. Extraction. Scanning a story to find discrete chunks of information encoded in it.

Benefits of Sense Making Through Extraction
- Extracting meaning from stories is a familiar analytical process that leads to limiting our sense-making activities to obvious and immediate fragments of meaning.
- Stories become tagged with meaning and become easier to remember and transmit to others because they are associated with stable associations of meaning.
- Group or individual dialogues engaged in sense making through extraction can be conducted more quickly than some other forms of sense making.

Pitfalls of Sense Making Through Extraction
- Stories are simplified in an effort to find and articulate clear sound bites of meaning.
- It is more likely that stories are left in isolation from one another. Meaning is construed from the story being analyzed. Relationships between multiple stories often do not enter into the discussion.
- Stories become abandoned carcasses of dead meaning. Once the key lessons are gleaned from a story, it may never be revisited again.

3. Projection. Passively allowing someone else to interpret or dictate the meaning of a story.

Benefits of Sense Making Through Projection
- People may struggle with making sense of their stories. Offering an interpretation may get the ball rolling and lead to more in-depth discussions.

- Projection is a good way to get listeners of a story involved in sense making. As each person projects his or her experiences, a web of meaning emerges. The diversity and energy of other people's story projections creates a stimulating environment of discovery.
- Through projection, themes relevant to a group can be associated with the story.

Pitfalls of Sense Making Through Projection
- People become lazy or dependent on others to provide meaning.
- People can be entrapped by other people's stories. When meaning is provided without the work, struggle, and uncertainty that is so often a part of the sense-making process, people might start living someone else's value system or reality.
- It can be gratifying and rewarding to provide meaning to others. It can be a seductive path of power whereby we set ourselves or others up as the seat of knowledge.

4. Insight. Sense making of story is a complex activity. Experiences from a varied set of domains and sources are reviewed with reflection and circumspection. Out of this internal and external dialogue of meaning, insights and epiphanies emerge.

Benefits of Sense Making Through Insight
- People gain deep, lasting perspectives.
- People are changed, and this is reflected in new behaviors.
- People become more empathetic toward others because they have richer and more varied understanding of themselves. They can connect more easily with others.

Pitfalls of Sense Making Through Insight
- This kind of sense making can be very draining and time-consuming.
- Insights do not usually come quickly or easily.
- This can be very scary for others. They are in uncharted territory and very vulnerable.
- Because sense making through insights is soul-searching in nature, people will dredge up emotionally heavy stuff from their pasts. Most facilitators are neither trained nor required to act as therapists.

Closing Thoughts on Sense Making with Stories for Facilitators

There are no simple rules to guiding sense-making processes. The more you become comfortable and confident in your abilities to be sensitive, aware, and reflective in the moment, the easier it will be to discern what is required in each situation. My style of facilitation teeters on the verge of chaos and vulnerability. I strive to push myself and others to enter into "emergent" forms of sense making with stories. I have had my share of failures, but more often than not I have been graced to watch purpose and heart unfold in new ways. This is deeply rewarding and always humbling.

I believe sense making with stories is the most sacred and demanding aspect of facilitation. It is the essence of what facilitation is all about. We are challenged to balance the competing drives for structure, security, certainty, and clarity with complexity, chaos, and soulfulness. In the end we must trust the process. Sense making with stories is a circular endeavor. Through stories and sense making, we participate in the endless cycle of creation and destruction. It is our call to being. Without stories and sense making, we are asleep, dead to ourselves and others.

Chapter Summary and Key Points

Whenever we work with stories, we are involved in sense making. Although there are different forms of sense making, we cannot apply all of them at once. Each person will have a different perspective, which adds to the richness of the experience. However, according to Professor Boje, emergent sense making yields the most powerful insights. We ended the chapter by reviewing four dynamics facilitators need to be aware of when working with people's stories. Part Two of the book provides detailed instructions for a collection of story-based activities aimed at helping people develop breakthrough communication skills.

Key Points

There are multiple forms of sense making.

- Reflective sense making that occurs in the "now" is called emergent.
- There are four dynamics that occur during sense making with stories that facilitators need to be aware of:

  Rationalizations

  Extraction

  Projection

  Insight

  - *Rationalization* occurs when we use stories to justify existing ideas, opinions, thoughts, emotions, or behaviors.

- *Extraction* occurs when we scan a story to find discrete chunks of information encoded in it.
- *Projection* occurs when we passively allow someone else to interpret or dictate the meaning of a story.
- *Insight* occurs when our experiences from a varied set of domains and sources are reviewed with reflection and circumspection. Out of this internal and external dialogue of meaning, insights and epiphanies emerge.
- There are no simple rules to guiding sense-making processes. The more you become comfortable and confident in your abilities to be sensitive, aware, and reflective in the moment, the easier it will be to discern what is required in each situation.

Part Two

Story-Based Activities for Developing Breakthrough Communication Skills

In Part One we reviewed techniques for how to work effectively with stories, introduced a tool for assessing story-based communication competencies, and explored the subtleties of sense-making with stories. Part Two offers a collection of activities for developing breakthrough communication skills. These activities can be woven into workshops, used during meetings, done as self-development exercises, or incorporated as new communication tools for existing business processes.

This introduction to Part Two includes two charts you can use to help you decide what activity is best suited for your needs. Even though Part Two is designed in a non-linear self-serve fashion, I encourage you to read all of the activities. They are not written as recipes to be blindly followed. These activities will give you an engaging preview of how you can experientially help others develop breakthrough communication skills. These are tried-and-true activities that have been a part of my practice as an executive coach and group process facilitator.

Structure of Activities

Every activity has the following structural elements:

Structural Element	*Description*
Background	Every activity begins with a short background story that describes how I developed, discovered, or learned about the activity.
Facilitation Level	The facilitation level for the activity (easy, moderate, or difficult).
Objectives	Three simple sentences that frame the purpose and goals of the activities.
Materials	A list of materials needed to run the activity.
Time	The amount of time required for the activity.
Directions	Straightforward numbered steps are provided to walk you through how to run the activity.
Debriefing	Advice is given on how to get the most out of the debriefing process at the conclusion of every activity. Questions with sample answers that relate back to the activity's objectives can be used to stimulate debriefing discussions.
Variations	List of ideas on how to vary the standard activity. Every activity can morph into many new ones by introducing additional variables or modifying one of the core ones.

Tips	Thorough tips on how to facilitate the activity, what to expect, how to respond to specific dynamics, and how to coach participants during the activity are offered.
Applications	Suggestions for different ways and organizational settings in which to use an activity. Activities do not have to be limited to workshop settings. Ideas are offered on how to weave activities into organization development activities and standard business processes.
Case Study	Each activity ends with a story of one of my experiences running it and lessons learned in the process.

Suggestions on How to Work with the Activities

Here are some suggestions on how to work with these activities:

1. Read through the activity several times.
2. Try the activity on your own.
3. Visualize yourself leading the activity.
4. Pilot the activity with a small group of people. Be clear with the group that this is your first time facilitating this activity. Obtain feedback from the group.
5. Incorporate people's feedback and suggestions.
6. Run the activity a few times.
7. Experiment with variations.
8. Put your personal touches on the activity and make it your own.

Some Common Concepts and Terms Used in Activities

Throughout the activities there are some common concepts and terms that appear over and over again. These terms may mean different things to different people so I have provided some guidance as to how I am using them and how they relate to stories and breakthrough communication skills.

Indexing

Stories are tagged with meta-data. Our experiences are stored in our minds as stories. Loosely speaking, these stories have labels associated with them. Facilitating with stories requires us to be aware of how stories are triggered. Many of the activities involve stimulating people's indexing schemes—sometimes to help them expand their index and at other times to help them use their index scheme to relate their story to other stories. When our experiences are well indexed, we are able to see connections and relationships more easily. A strong index functions like a hub. New experiences and other people's stories can be quickly plugged in. See Chapter 2's discussion of the Communication Competency Model for more details on indexing.

Frame of Reference
Stories are the lens through which we see the world. In the context of stories, a frame of reference can be thought of as a collection of stories that contributes to create a domain of knowing or perception. Working with stories can enable people to move through different frames of reference. Someone else's experiences, shared as stories, allow me to see the world in a different way. Likewise, stories are used to construct compelling representations of knowledge that have the power to shift people's perspectives. Whether stated or not, most of the activities invoke the power of stories to create some sort of frame of reference. This is the active playground on which breakthrough communication occurs.

Linkages and Associations
Stories in isolation are of limited value. Emergent sense-making (see Chapter 3) is engaged by the interaction and inter-relationship between stories. Lots of the activities involve asking people to look for the linkages or connections and associations between their stories and the stories of others. The richness of stories and the insights to be gained are produced by the crisscrossing pattern of stories being related to one another. This lies at the heart of what many of these exercises attempt to experientially give to participants.

Active Listening
Per our discussion in Chapter 1, stories require active listening (see the nine functions of stories). Developing breakthrough communication skills depends on active listening. The Communication Competency Model explained in Chapter 2 is centered on the multi-faceted nature and dynamics of active listening. These activities are intended to give people a taste of this kind of deep listening.

Guidelines for Selecting an Activity
Activities are organized alphabetically by name. Following are two summary tables to help you select the activity best suited for your needs. Table 1 relates the activity to one of the three rings of the story-based Communication Competency Model (see Chapter 2 for more detail), lists the objectives of the activity, rates the difficulty of facilitating the activity, and gives an estimate of how much time is required for the activity.

Table 2 puts the applications and objectives of an exercise side-by-side to aid you in finding the right activity.

Table 1. Activities in Relation to the Communication Competency Model

Activity	Relationship to Ring from Competency Model	Objectives	Difficulty	Time
Children's Book	Core	Develop and strengthen powers of observation. Instill openness and receptivity to new perspectives. Increase focus and concentration.	Easy	20 min.
Concepts Made Easy	Interaction	Utilize analogies and metaphors to explain ideas and concepts to others. Increase sensitivity to other people's vocabulary and knowledge. Communicate complex thoughts, feeling, and ideas through stories.	Easy	15 to 30 min.
Cookie Jar	Process	Recall significant recent stories and reflect on them. Relate stories to topics being discussed. Provide learning prompts to expand discussion and visit multiple people's perspectives on it.	Moderate	Up to 3 or 4 minutes per person in the group
Expand/Collapse	Interaction	Adjust the amount of detail when telling a story. Develop situational awareness to determine what details to include and how much. Transform long stories into succinct sound bites.	Easy	15 to 30 min.

Continued

Table 1. *Continued*

Activity	Relationship to Ring from Competency Model	Objectives	Difficulty	Time
Guided Journey	Core	Engage the imagination to envision new possibilities. Use a collaborative storytelling process to stimulate reflection. Uncover organizational and personal challenges and stimulate creative solutions.	Difficult	60+ min.
Listening as an Ally	Core	Experience listening to someone's story without rendering judgment. Expand your ability to provide the support a speaker might need to express him/herself fully, honestly, and authentically. Generate compassion for yourself (as listener) and the speaker.	Moderate	30 to 45 min.
Magic Three	Process	Provide a structured activity to guide people through an experience of reflection. Practice authentic communication. Create a connection with listeners.	Easy	Up to 15 min. per person
Mirror	Core	Use stories to communicate multiple perspectives. Practice entering other people's frames of reference to understand multiple perspectives. Generate out-of-the-box thinking that takes into account multiple perspectives.	Moderate	45 to 60 min.

Random Conversation	Interaction	Help people experience how stories can be triggered by any stimuli. Practice selecting relevant experiences to share when communicating. Develop the ability to scan new information and find personal connections.	Moderate	15 to 30 min.
Relic	Interaction	Create a safe and fun vehicle for people to share something personal. Use an object to trigger stories. Gain insight into stories that have had a formative impact on us.	Easy	3 min. per person
Stories in Words	Process	Use words to trigger stories and connections. Increase awareness of how words can be used to index stories. Encourage associations and linkages between people and ideas.	Moderate	30 to 45 min.
Story Collage™	Process	Help people discover and organize their stories. Reflect on stories and look for relationships between them. Promote dialogue, sharing, and learning from each other's stories.	Easy	15 to 90 min.

Continued

Table 1. *Continued*

Activity	Relationship to Ring from Competency Model	Objectives	Difficulty	Time
Story Scrap Booking	Process	Create a conversation piece to encourage open communication. Capture key stories to examine the connections between them and transfer knowledge. Use stories to promote self-awareness and active sense making.	Moderate	60 to 90 min.
Study Tour	Core	Become aware of how perceptions are formed. Generate alternative interpretations of observations. Engage in dialogue to verify and expand initial perceptions.	Difficult	60 min.
Take Three	Core	Create a space of listening that slows people down. Penetrate below the surface to hear new shades of meaning. Participate in a dialogue invigorated by deep listening.	Easy	30 to 45 min.
Three Channels	Core	Develop stronger active listening skills by capturing and deciphering three channels of information. Synthesize information from multiple channels to draw conclusions and guide communications with others. Connect with others on a deeper and more fundamental level.	Difficult	45 min.

Table 2.   Applications and Objectives of the Activities

Activity	Applications	Objectives
Children's Book	Use with groups who will be responsible for reviewing or updating documents. Incorporate a variation of this activity with internal and external marketing focus groups. Include this activity during supervisory and managerial training sessions. Time permitting, do the activity in two parts. First run it the basic way using children's books. Run it a second time using a piece of an organizational policy or procedure manual.	• *Develop and strengthen powers of observations.* • *Instill openness and receptivity to new perspectives.* • *Increase focus and concentration.*
Concepts Made Easy	Audit existing workshops and courses to make sure they incorporate enough analogies/metaphors into the materials. Provide practice sessions and coaching to technical people who need to make presentations to and influence decision makers who lack their knowledge.	• *Utilize analogies and metaphors to explain ideas and concepts to others.* • *Increase sensitivity of other people's vocabulary and knowledge.* • *Communicate complex thoughts, feeling, and ideas through stories.*

Continued

Table 2. *Continued*

Activity	Applications	Objectives
Cookie Jar	Use this activity for multi-day offsite retreats. Run an abbreviated version of this activity at longer meetings (e.g., a strategic planning meeting). Before wrapping up a meeting (but don't do this as the very last activity), ask people to jot down their stories on index cards. The meeting facilitator can run through the cards quickly to reinforce and validate things that have surfaced. It is also a good way to gauge feelings or perspectives that may have been missed during the meeting. I have had organizations select and post a few of the stories from the index cards on intranets (or other web-based collaborative documents and spaces) for others to have a vicarious account of the meeting. Incorporate this activity into an after action review process for project teams. Weave this activity into other project management processes or meetings.	• *Recall significant recent stories and reflect on them.* • *Relate stories to topics being discussed.* • *Provide learning prompts to expand discussion and visit multiple people's perspectives on it.*
Expand/Collapse	Include this activity in presentation skills workshops. Incorporate this as a skill-building activity during a project team's kickoff meeting. Put in place some practices and standards for sharing stories. Use this activity to mentor leaders. Help them to understand how to leverage their personal and organizational stories in a variety of settings.	• *Adjust the amount of detail when telling a story.* • *Develop situational awareness to determine what details to include and how much.* • *Transform long stories into succinct sound bites.*

Guided Journey	When a group becomes stuck, use guided visualizations as a way of stimulating creative thinking and idea generation.	• Engage the imagination to envision new possibilities.
	Incorporate guided visualization during strategic planning retreats.	• Use a collaborative storytelling process to stimulate reflection.
	Use guided visualization with change management steering groups to help them imagine the impact of the proposed change on all the stakeholders.	• Uncover organizational and personal challenges and stimulate creative solutions.
	Add guided visualization to any type of workshop during which you want to encourage stress management, personal growth, or reflection.	
Listening as an Ally	If you facilitate meetings, you can use this activity to evaluate the meeting using the topic: "What did you feel or think about this meeting?"	• Experience listening to someone's story without rendering judgment.
	In coaching sessions (as coach), you can apply the repetitive question technique to elicit content before exploring the coachee's experience in more detail.	• Expand your ability to provide the support a speaker might need to express him/herself fully, honestly, and authentically.
	As a journaling activity, you can ask yourself the repetitive question.	• Generate compassion for yourself (as listener) and the speaker.
Magic Three	This is a great activity to use in any offsite retreat.	• Provide a structured activity to guide people through an experience of reflection.
	Incorporate this as a team-building activity or let members of a team take turns sharing their magic three at the start of regular meetings.	• Practice authentic communication.
	Use as an icebreaker or lunch activity during an event.	• Create a connection with listeners.

Continued

Table 2. *Continued*

Activity	Applications	Objectives
Mirror	Incorporate this activity into customer service training programs. Run through the activity and then repeat a variation of it using customer service stories. Use this activity to help salespeople learn how to enter a customer's frame of reference to anticipate and appreciate a customer's needs, concerns, and questions. Customize a version of this activity process as an intervention and communication tool for people who are going through change management events involving mergers, acquisitions, or any reorganization initiatives.	• *Use stories to communicate multiple perspectives.* • *Practice entering other people's frames of reference to understand multiple perspectives.* • *Generate out-of-the-box thinking that takes into account multiple perspectives.*
Random Conversation	Use this activity in employee orientation programs to break the ice and give people an opportunity to share something personal in a safe manner. Great interactive activity for town hall meetings when new announcements are being made. Build in time for people in smaller groups to react to the announcement by sharing their organizational experiences that relate to the information being disseminated. Whenever possible, build in time for people to share some of these with the whole assembly. Incorporate a variation of this activity during strategic brainstorming sessions.	• *Help people experience how stories can be triggered by any stimuli.* • *Practice selecting relevant experiences to share when communicating.* • *Develop the ability to scan new information and find personal connections.*

Relic	This is a great team-building activity that can be used in a variety of situations. Incorporate the activity as part of a project kickoff meeting. Use this activity at the beginning of a standing meeting. This even works for virtual meetings (e.g., conference calls, or web-based formats).	• *Create a safe and fun vehicle for people to share something personal.* • *Use an object to trigger stories.* • *Gain insight into stories that have had a formative impact on us.*
Stories in Words	Incorporate this activity into employee orientation and board of directors' initiation programs. I've videotaped senior leaders of the organization sharing their key words and stories. It also makes a great follow-up discussion to ask people to describe the new role they are assuming and how they see themselves supporting the organization's mission through it. Make these stories available on an intranet site. Be sure to give people the ability to add their comments or stories. Do this activity every year as the open part of an organization's strategic planning meeting. Use this activity during marketing focus groups conducted with external customers.	• *Use words to trigger stories and connections.* • *Increase awareness of how words can be used to index stories.* • *Encourage associations and linkages between people and ideas.*
Story Collage™	Incorporate Story Collage™ into business processes (e.g., performance review, after-action reviews, employee orientation, product development, and marketing focus groups). Instill standard story sharing, dialogue, and reflection with groups. Harvest key stories to promote knowledge sharing.	• *Help people discover and organize their stories.* • *Reflect on stories and look for relationships between them.* • *Promote dialogue, sharing, and learning from each other's stories.*

Continued

Introduction to Part Two **63**

Table 2. *Continued*

Activity	Applications	Objectives
Story Scrap Booking	Incorporate this activity as a part of a team retreat. Use this as a group process during after-action reviews for large-scale projects or end-of-year discussions. It's an excellent tool for promoting knowledge transfer. Weave a variation of this activity into strategic planning processes.	*• Create a conversation piece to encourage open communication.* *• Capture key stories to examine the connections between them and transfer knowledge.* *• Use stories to promote self-awareness and active sense-making.*
Study Tour	Lunch-time activity for any type of workshop. Include this activity in any customer service/call center/help desk learning event. Give this activity as a homework assignment in advance of product development or marketing brainstorming meetings. These study tours should involve products and customers to be discussed during this meeting. Begin the meeting by listening to people's observations.	*• Become aware of how perceptions are formed.* *• Generate alternative interpretations of observations.* *• Engage in dialogue to verify and expand initial perceptions.*
Take Three	On a regular basis, record part of a meeting. Randomly select a two-minute sound byte to play at the next meeting. Start the meeting with this activity as a way of getting people focused and tuned in to each other. It's critical to set strong ground rules of minimal analysis and whatever is replayed mustn't be used as fodder during the current meeting. In other words, people are not allowed to take anything from the sound byte out of context to serve their own needs. Incorporate this activity into team-building workshops and senior leadership retreats.	*• Create a space of listening that slows people down.* *• Penetrate below the surface to hear new shades of meaning.* *• Participate in a dialogue invigorated by deep listening.*

Three Channels

Build this activity as a key component of almost any program, especially customer service, sales, and supervisor training.

Establish this practice of active listening during workshops, retreats, and other professional development activities; then use this technique to facilitate conflict resolutions.

Whenever a problem is going to be presented during any type of meeting, ask the group to share its observations of the three channels of information before moving into any other phase of the discussion.

· Develop stronger active listening skills by capturing and deciphering three channels of information.
· Synthesize information from multiple channels to draw conclusions and guide communications with others.
· Connect with others on a deeper and more fundamental level.

Invitation

I am forever amazed at how much I learn every time I run these activities. Despite hundreds of experiences in very different settings, I am picking up new things all the time. I'd like to invite each of you to share your experiences of using these activities with me. With your permission, I will periodically post what you share with me on my website so that others can also benefit from what you have learned. Feel free to write or call me with your questions. I will always do my best to get back to you as quickly as I can.

It's a thrill to share these activities with you, and I can't wait to hear your experiences. Here's how to contact me:

Terrence L. Gargiulo

(781) 894–4381

Email: terrence@makingstories.net

Web: www.makingstories.net or www.oncloudnine.org

Children's Book

Children's Book

Background

My face dropped when Gabriel, my three-year-old son, handed me the *Lorax* by Dr. Seuss to read for the umpteenth time. I did my best parental redirect, "Gabriel, we haven't read *Night Kitchen* in a while; how about that?" Not a little man to lose sight of his goals, he brought me back to task. With a sigh to myself, I opened the book, settled into a good snuggle with my son, and began reading the story. On this occasion, I had a mind-opening experience. The anticipated monotony of the story was replaced with fresh eyes and excitement. I saw details in the pictures I had never seen. The story attached itself to new associations, and what had become mundane opened up into a whole new world.

Facilitation Level
Easy

Objectives
1. Develop and strengthen powers of observation.
2. Instill openness and receptivity to new perspectives.
3. Increase focus and concentration.

Materials
- Children's books—half as many as total number of participants

Time
20 minutes

Directions
1. Get a handful of children's book, one book for every two people.
2. Break the group into pairs and give each pair a book.
3. One person reads the book out loud to his or her partner.
4. Then ask the pairs to switch roles and reread the book.

5. Instruct pairs to thumb through the book together, pointing out things they observed on the second reading. Pairs should also look for new observations while they are paging through the book.

6. Debrief

Debriefing

- I've observed a weird phenomenon with this activity. People will initially get excited when they observe new details. During the debriefing, people will trivialize their experience. They have a jaded moment of disappointment when they realize that the results of the activity are a truism they already know. For some it will stop there. For these people, keep things light and move on. Some people will become committed to bringing the activity's practice of mindful observation into other areas of their lives. These people will see the merit. Use this as an invitation to explore mindfulness in more detail. I'll encourage people to try little activities like looking people in the eyes or noticing the name of a store clerk and thanking the person by name. I always refer people to a wonderful book by Tich Nhat Hahn called *The Miracle of Mindfulness.*

- Draw people into a discussion about the advantages and drawbacks of observing things in a stable way. Stability enables us to navigate the world in a repeatable and known way. Without it, we would stumble. Limiting the world and our relationships to sustaining stable, known structures deadens our sensibilities to the dynamism around us. Good communication demands that we not limit our interactions with others to what we expect to hear. Our challenge is to say fresh and engaged. We cannot afford to ever stop re-encountering the world.

- *What's the relationship between good powers of observation and communication?* If we are not tuned in to the thoughts, moods, feelings, and needs of others, our communications will fall short. Good powers of observation provide us with raw data to adjust what we communicate and how we communicate it. Observation skills are listening skills. We need to become like pitchforks that, when placed in proximity to one another, alter the frequency at which they vibrate to match the other.

Variations

- Ask people to bring books from home.
- Read the book out loud to the group three times with three different readers. After the second and third readings, give people two minutes to record observations.
- Work in groups of three or four.

- Have each pair or group read the same book.

- Read a story with no pictures to the whole group (e.g., short story or folktale). Make sure the story is 1,200 words or less. Read the story only twice.

- Do the activity with only pictures. Select a picture book—a children's book or a book of photography. Start all the pairs or groups at the same time. Depending on how many pictures and the complexity of the pictures, give people ten to twenty-five seconds to look at each picture. Act as the timer and strike a glass with a utensil after each ten-to-twenty-five-second interval. You can do this with the whole group, using a projector and a slide show of pictures. On other occasions I have invited people to bring in photos to share.

- Hand out a brochure or some organizational collateral that people are familiar with. Give them ten minutes to reread it on their own and record their observations. Then break them into pairs to share their findings for five minutes. Do a short debriefing with the whole group.

Tips

- If there are any parents in the group, they will immediately relate to the activity. However, don't get carried away with the parent angle and become insensitive to people without children. If there are very few parents with young children in the group, consider doing one of the activity variations that use pictures.

- Avoid overly simplistic children's books.

- It's more difficult to run this activity as one group. You will need to jump-start the conversation. People will be reluctant to share any observations. People are cautious and self-critical. They don't want other people to think they missed a detail in the story that others saw. Offer an observation to start the conversation.

- This is a good activity to use when you want something light and easy to do with a group. Insights gained from this activity are not trivial, but on the surface it's a good way to give a group a break and have some fun. I've been known to hand out cookies and milk before doing this activity.

- If you use a children's book in the activity, be prepared to discuss why. A children's book appears so straightforward and yet it is filled with discovery opportunities. People know if they re-watch a movie or reread a major piece of literature, they expect to learn new things, but in their minds a children's book isn't in the same category. However, nothing could be further from the truth. Help people to see that we all walk around blind or with thick eyeglasses tinted with our assumptions and expectations. Because of its juvenile appearance, and how quickly we are prone to dismiss it as something that does not require our full attention, a children's book helps accentuate this point.

Everything needs and deserves our undivided attention. Good communication cannot occur without it.

Applications

1. Use with groups who will be responsible for reviewing or updating documents.
2. Use a variation of this activity with internal and external marketing focus groups.
3. Include this activity during supervisory and managerial training sessions. Time permitting, do the activity in two parts. First run it the basic way using children's books. Run it a second time using a piece of an organizational policy or procedure manual.

Case Study

A major company had hired me to help it collect stories from customers and employees to beef up its collateral. The champion of the project was far removed from the people who were going to be impacted the most by my work, so I decided to try to build a coalition of support for my efforts. I met with middle and senior managers of the marketing and communications area. I tried to forego too many formalities and dove straight into this activity. When I handed out a bunch of Dr. Seuss books, I thought people were going to strangle me. It was bad enough that a crazy story expert was going to tell them how to do their jobs. Asking people to take time out of their busy schedules to read children's books was adding insult to injury. Most people grumbled their way through the activity. Given the energy and attitudes in the room, the activity appeared to be a failure until I started pointing out details that had escaped their attention. The environment became a mix of competitiveness, with people jumping in to outdo me and each other with their observations, and a growing realization that there must be some method to my madness. Before the energy waned, I took out a pile of key corporate collaterals, including annual reports and marketing brochures. I put people in teams of four and asked them to read through these collaterals with fresh eyes. It worked like a charm. Each group came up with a great collection of observations that translated into improvements. When I debriefed the groups' work, it naturally led us to a discussion of how stories could be used more effectively. People began sharing some organizational stories that they wanted to incorporate into collaterals. We ended the session by discussing some of the ways they might begin to collect these stories on a regular basis.

Concepts Made Easy

Concepts Made Easy

Background

I was teaching my first writing class at a major defense contractor. I was struggling with how to help people communicate in clear, simple ways. As technical people, they were prone to lengthy and detailed descriptions of their projects. I wanted them to become more comfortable communicating with people who knew little or nothing about their area of expertise and who had no interest in hearing all of the details. I tried a two-step approach. First, I had them write instructions for making a peanut butter and jelly sandwich for an alien visiting our planet. I wanted them to see that no matter how careful and thorough they tried to be, they would end up making assumptions about their readers. Writing bullet-proof instructions for all audiences is impossible. It was hysterical to see the wide range and type of details included in the directions. The second part of the assignment was to take a difficult technical concept from their areas of expertise and find an analogy or metaphor to explain it so that a ten-year-old could understand. The group was not too impressed with either me or my assignment. I had a moment or two of self-doubt, but I ignored their resistance and explained to them that going through this assignment would help them become better writers. It did! While they agonized over finding a suitable analogy or metaphor, once they did they were blown away at how easy it was to describe even complicated concepts.

Facilitation Level
Easy

Objectives
1. Utilize analogies and metaphors to explain ideas and concepts to others.
2. Increase sensitivity to other people's vocabulary and knowledge.
3. Communicate complex thoughts, feeling, and ideas through stories.

Materials
- Index cards with topics (see Step 1)
- Technical summary for each topic

Time
Ten to thirty minutes

Directions

1. Create a stack of index cards with technical topics. The fields of science, technology, or medicine are good places to find topics. For example, I have cards with terms like photosynthesis, entropy, computer programming with service-oriented architectures, and dialysis.

2. In case people are unfamiliar with the topic, provide a one-page technical summary of it for them to read.

3. Divide the group into pairs and provide each pair with an index card and summary sheet.

4. Instruct each pair to come up with an analogy or metaphor that even a ten-year-old could understand.

5. Debrief the activity.

Debriefing

- For an analogy/metaphor to be effective, it does not have to be a perfect match. In fact, it is neither necessary nor desirable. Many times the communication richness comes from the incongruence between what you are trying to explain and the analogy/metaphor. When the concept and analogy/metaphor do not match perfectly, they become an opportunity to fill in the details. As long as you grab people's imaginations with something they know, it is much easier to complete the picture with all the missing details.

- *How do analogies and metaphors change your communication style?* We become less didactic. We can communicate more quickly, effectively, and interactively when we use analogies and metaphors. It takes less time to cover the same amount of information. Analogies and metaphors build bridges between people. Less becomes more and people are apt to become more engaged. Encourage people to be more conscious of using them in conversations.

- *How do analogies and metaphors affect listeners?* Listeners are more attentive. It is easier for someone to work with analogies and metaphors because they encapsulate more information. Listeners can decode them and manipulate them as chunks of information. Conversations are more exciting because exploring and discovering become part of the natural rhythm.

- *Why is it so difficult to come up with a good analogy or metaphor?* Analogies and metaphors demonstrate a very thorough knowledge and command of a concept, idea, or emotion. It's been said that the easiest way to assess someone's level of knowledge is to ask him or her to explain something to another person. However, explaining is not enough. We might have command of the information, but the ability to translate it into a workable metaphor and analogy indicates that we have integrated the information into a network of associated links of knowledge. While it might be difficult, becoming more adept at using analogies and metaphors increases our communication and learning skills.

Variations

- Instead of using index cards, ask people to describe some aspect of their profession or hobby using an analogy or metaphor.
- During a lecture portion of a workshop, pause and ask someone to provide an analogy or metaphor to illustrate what you are explaining.
- Use this as an extemporaneous activity during a multi-day event. Pull out an index card at random and ask a member of the group to provide an analogy. This works best if the person already knows the concept and feels comfortable with it.
- Try the activity as a written one.
- Turn the activity into a contest. Time the group and see how many different analogies or metaphors they can come up. For this to work properly, the concept should be rich enough to yield lots of them.
- If one of the listeners in the pairs is naïve about the concept, when you debrief the group at large ask this listener to provide an explanation to the whole group to assess the effectiveness of the pair discussion.
- To move this activity from concepts to feelings, try playing a short clip from a movie. Then ask participants to explain the scene and the underlying emotions being portrayed by the actors with an analogy or metaphor.
- Introduce the effectiveness of analogies/metaphors at the beginning of a workshop or session. Invite people to track and record how many you used. After a break, compare people's notes to see how many analogies/metaphors they noticed. Use this as an opportunity to discuss how well they worked. Ask people to comment on how an analogy/metaphor affected their understanding.

Tips

- Practice, practice, practice. . . . The best way to help people become more aware of using analogies and metaphors more often is to be very good at it yourself and to model it all the time.
- Be willing to let people struggle. Finding an analogy/metaphor can be a difficult and lengthy process. Avoid the temptation to offer suggestions too quickly.

- Don't let people get too hung up on the difference between an analogy and metaphor. There is a difference between them and serious students of language will take issue with your laissez faire attitude, but for the purposes of this activity it is not important and can become a tangent that takes the group off course.
- Develop a one-page list of your favorite examples of effective analogies/metaphors. Whenever possible, tailor these examples for your audience.

Applications
1. Audit existing workshops and courses to make sure they incorporate enough analogies/metaphors into the materials.
2. Provide practice sessions and coaching to technical people who need to make presentations to and influence decision makers who lack their knowledge.

Case Study

I was heading a team of instructional designers and trainers to create an information technology orientation program for global senior human resources executives of a Fortune 10 company. Conversations with stakeholders had already alerted me to the reality that almost all of these executives had little to no technical background. Even worse, one of the chief reasons behind the program's creation was the impatient and intolerant attitude these executives exhibited toward information technology. Before the project kickoff meeting with my team, I made a long list of technical terms and concepts. After some introductory activities with the team, I broke them up into groups and gave each group a list of technical terms. I instructed them to come up with analogies and metaphors apropos to the company and human resources concepts. We wove these examples into all of the materials and created a cheat book for trainers with all of the metaphors and analogies in it. After we ran the first program, the evaluations were filled with comments about how the course materials and trainers had made technical mumbo jumbo so easy to understand and fun to learn. I got my greatest satisfaction when I was walking the down the halls one day and I heard one of the executives explaining a technical concept with one of the analogies my team had written.

Cookie Jar

Cookie Jar

Background

I always like to spend time at the beginning of a multi-day workshop reflecting on the previous day. I had been working with a quiet group that was full of insights and willing to share, but reserved. It was the third day of the workshop and the last two morning debriefings had started very slowly. I was feeling tired and I was not sure if I could get them going. I spontaneously decided to try something different to get everyone's juices flowing. There was a large cookie jar with a handful of cookies left in it and a pile of index cards next to it. I took a handful of cookies and shoved them into my mouth and muttered some joke about forgetting to get a cup of coffee. I offered others the remaining cookies while I handed out index cards. I instructed everyone to write down a description of a story they remembered hearing from the previous day and to throw it in the cookie jar. Maybe it was the increase in my blood sugar, but my idea worked like a charm. We had an excellent debriefing. After two hours I had to insist on a morning break because no one wanted to end our discussion.

Facilitation Level
Moderate

Objectives
1. Recall significant recent stories and reflect on them.
2. Relate stories to topics being discussed.
3. Provide learning prompts to expand discussion and visit multiple people's perspectives on it.

Materials
- An index card for each person
- A cookie jar or other container

Time
Allot up to three or four minutes per person

Directions

1. Give index cards to everyone.

2. Instruct people to write down short descriptions of a story they remember from the previous day's discussion.

3. Put the index cards in a jar or some other container and draw them out at random.

4. Ask the person who wrote the index card to share the story with the group. Have him or her expand on why this story stuck out in his or her mind and how the story relates to the topics being covered.

5. Invite others to share their thoughts.

Debriefing

- Once a story has been related to the learning themes of your event, use it as an opportunity to delve deeper into that subject. Revisiting a story naturally promotes discovery. New insights will emerge and people can internalize analytical realizations.

- Once a story has been shared, it's okay for the group to be analytical. The story is being used to invigorate people's imaginations so that they can engage their heads to look for relationships and learning and to decipher new strands of meaning.

- Allow people to connect stories together. Behind every story is another story. When a story resonates with someone, there's a good chance he or she has a similar or related story. Although these may feel tangential, they can be greater facilitators of unexpected learning.

- *How do stories change the debriefing process?* Stories create a community. Stories prevent people from becoming isolated. When I share an insight in the form of a didactic statement, it is abstract, and while it may be similar to someone else's learning, its impact is localized. The insight is treated as an intellectual curiosity to be mulled over by ourselves and by others. We are separated from our insight by virtue of our intellectual manipulation of it and, while it may be noticed by others, it is unlikely to mean much to them. Stories challenge our assumptions and force us to look beyond the surface of things. Stories move our imaginations. Debriefings that focus on key stories shared the previous day will be vibrant and full of possibilities. People should feel more engaged by the discussion. Individuals are transformed into a community of collaborating learners. With stories, we give each other permission to be guides and coaches as we make sense of our world.

- *Why do certain stories resonate more with us than others do?* One of the things I love most about this activity is that people realize how strong an impression their stories can make. It's wonderful feedback when someone recounts an experience we shared with the group and reveals how our story affected them. Then the whole group chimes in with their two cents' worth. Suddenly we are learning stars blazing the trails of new frontiers. It's a neat feeling and it's one of the things that get people coming back for more and more stories. Why one story resonates with us versus another is a very individual thing. Asking the question will help us understand our relationship to a story. Penetrating the significance of a story leads us to personal insights. We may find ourselves in a field of personal experiences that we have never mined for insights.

Variations

- Hand out the index cards at the end of the day and have people write down their stories before they leave.

- Have people draw someone else's card at random. See whether they can reconstruct the story and what the story means to them.

- Given the time this activity takes (up to five minutes or sometimes even more per person), select as many stories as your timeline will allow. Be sure to set this expectation. Hand-select the index cards you feel will yield the best discussions.

- Summarize the cards as a group. See how many people remembered the same story.

- Put up butcher paper with the previous day's major themes. Instead of index cards, give people large sticky pads on which to record their stories. Then ask people to post their stories on the butcher paper under the theme that best describes the learning theme present in their stories. Have people stand around the pieces of butcher paper and discuss their stories.

- After people have written their stories down on index cards, give them twenty minutes to stand up and walk around the room sharing their stories and hearing other people's stories. Build in some time for large group debriefing.

- After people have written their stories down on index cards, break them into small groups (between four and six people) to discuss their stories. Instruct them to be prepared to report out to the whole group key findings and the relationship between everyone's stories in their group.

- Work in pairs and then do a short debriefing with the whole group.

- Work in groups of three. Designate one person to act as a facilitator. The facilitator's job is to ask questions, probe, and look for the relationships between the stories and learning themes.

- Use this technique for debriefing any smaller group activity that involves people discussing their experience.

Tips
- This activity requires participant collaboration. If the previous day's activities did not include lots of opportunities for people to share their experiences, then this activity will not work. You should use another debriefing technique.
- Before doing this activity, be sure you are encouraging people to share their stories. When someone shares a story, flag it as such and bring it to the group's attention. Say something like, "Thanks, John. That's a great story." This will help people recognize stories and make it easier to recall them when you do the activity.
- Be prepared with examples. If you are running a multi-day event, do one morning debriefing without stories and one with stories. On the first day, while others are reflecting on what was memorable, share stories that stick out in your mind. See whether you can elicit stories from others.
- If more than one person recalls the same story, be prepared to spend time exploring people's associations with it.
- If you have a full agenda, you may need to limit the time for this activity (but budget as much time as you can). Debriefing the previous day with a group is one of my favorite activities. Some of my most memorable interactions with groups occur during this time. Once the ball gets rolling, it's hard to stop. When the discussion is rich, it leads to new topics. I have been known to cut planned activities from a workshop to allow a good discussion. If you want to cut an activity, give the group a choice or reset people's expectations.
- Visually capture the stories as they are shared. Sometimes I'll draw or ask someone in the group to draw a key image associated with a story. The stories become anchors for people. As new stories and learning occur, relate them back to these anchors. This allows you to create a tapestry of learning. It's a story line that encapsulates the learning experience. Everyone can refer back to these key stories to re-experience the event and reflect.

Applications
1. Use this activity for multi-day offsite retreats.
2. Run an abbreviated version of this activity at longer meetings (e.g., a strategic planning meeting). Before wrapping up a meeting (but don't do this as the very last activity), ask people to jot down their stories on index cards. The meeting facilitator can run through the cards quickly to reinforce and validate

Cookie Jar **83**

things that have surfaced. It is also a good way to gauge feelings or perspectives that may have been missed during the meeting. I have had organizations select and post a few of the stories from the index cards on intranets (or other web-based collaborative documents and spaces) for others to have a vicarious account of the meeting.

3. Incorporate this activity into an after-action review process for project teams. Weave this activity into other project management processes or meetings.

Case Study

John was a reserved management consultant who had spoken very little during the four-day communication skills workshop I was leading. I concluded he was being cautious with the group because he was a new employee. On the third morning, I ran the Cookie Jar activity. After I collected all of the index cards, I asked John to reach in the cookie jar and select the first one. He paused for a moment and had an odd look on his face. Then he said, "Whoever wrote this card is referring to a story I told yesterday." At this point, six people from the group said, "That must be my index card." John's expression went from confused to surprise.

John had told a story about when he was working as a contractor at the company where he was now employed and the difficult time he had when communicating with one of the employees. Being on the road a lot and not always near a computer, John telephoned this employee with all his questions and requests. In an effort to respect her time, John said he spent sometimes ten or fifteen minutes preparing for the call to make sure he had captured all of the things he needed to communicate. Every time he spoke to her, he felt more and more resistance and anger. She always seemed overwhelmed by his verbal communications. This confused John because she struck him as smart and capable and others spoke highly of her. She began to insist that John not call her, but instead email her with his questions. This irked John because it was easier for him to call. According to John, it became a battle. He dug his heels in deeper. After all, she was supposed to be supporting him. John was a contractor, so every minute of his time was billable. He was trying to save the company money. John said he felt entitled. Despite the fact he knew she wanted him to communicate via email, he wanted to communicate in the manner best suited to him—regardless of its impact on her. John said he finally acquiesced. The result was nothing short of miraculous. She began getting back to him quickly and always with excellent well-thought-out responses. An almost non-existent working relationship became a central one to John's success. John said his attitude is what had gotten him in trouble. He had not put her needs first, despite the fact that he knew what she wanted.

Despite his quiet nature, John's story had struck a chord with many people. Some people even knew the person in question and thanked John for helping them to understand why they were struggling with this person. The conversation was rousing. As people shared their experiences triggered by John's story, it naturally led to new learning themes. People sighed with their newfound realization about the importance of being sensitive to others' needs and putting those first when communicating. And John became integrated with the group in a way he had not expected. His story paved the way to accelerate a new collection of personal relationships.

Expand and Collapse

Expand and Collapse

Background

I had just facilitated an all-hands meeting for five hundred employees. The agenda included eliciting stories from employees regarding the rollout of a new product line. I was glowing from an event well run as I packed up my stuff when one of the senior vice presidents of the company came over to speak with me. "Listen, Terrence, this story stuff you do works great. I've got a challenge for you though. Is there any way to cut down the amount of time the process takes? Not all of the stories shared today were relevant, and some of them went on longer than necessary. I want to use storytelling as a process for other meetings, but I can't afford the amount of time it takes. Do you have any ideas?" He had a good point. I realized that since I love stories I was not always sensitive to the amount of time it can take for people to tell their stories. I nodded my head and told him I thought I had some ideas on how to help people tell their stories more succinctly.

Facilitation Level
Easy

Objectives
1. Adjust the amount of detail when telling a story.
2. Develop situational awareness to determine what details to include and how much.
3. Transform long stories into succinct sound bites.

Materials
- None

Time
Fifteen to thirty minutes

Directions
1. Ask people to write lists of some of their favorite movies and books.
2. Instruct them to select one from the list.

3. Give people five minutes to prepare a one-minute or less version of the story.

4. Break people into pairs and have them share their stories.

5. Debrief the activity.

Debriefing

- *Is anything lost when we tell an abbreviated version of our story?* One of the key reasons to tell a story is to elicit stories from others. Our story needs to be rich enough to stimulate other people's stories. People are not concerned with the completeness of our story. Details important to us are not important to others. We love the details because each one is packed with memories, feelings, and sensations. Feeling uncomfortable with leaving out details of our stories is natural. Story as performance thrives on vivid details because we are entertaining people. Using stories to facilitate communication requires us to provide just enough detail to be clear and evocative at the same time.

- *What cues should you be aware of when sharing a story?* Being aware of time is essential. Large formal group settings require us to be brief. The story has to be an engaging capsule that spurs others to tell their stories. On the other hand, if you are leading a group you have more leeway. Intimate settings also allow for longer stories. As a general rule, give others the opportunity to speak first. There are times when you need to jumpstart a conversation, but whenever possible listening to other people, demonstrating that you understand what they communicated will win you a hearing. If you wait, you may not need to truncate your story or you may pick up a cue as to the most effective way to share your story.

Variations

- Vary the amount of time people have to tell their stories.

- Do the activity as a group with people taking turns. If time is short, you do not need to have everyone do the activity.

- Randomize the amount of time people have to tell their stories. Until people are going to tell their stories they will not know how long they have. Use increments of thirty seconds (ranging from thirty seconds to three minutes).

- Try other story topics. Movies and books are a good way to get people started because they are structured stories, but anything that triggers a story will work. Remember the end goal—you want people to become adept at adjusting the amount of detail in the personal stories they tell.

- Use the activity on the spot during a discussion. After someone shares a story, ask him or her to either expand or collapse the amount of detail.

- Set up the activity as a ground rule. Any time a story is shared, participants can be asked to retell the story with more or less detail.

- Give people target audiences for their stories. For example, tell them their stories are being shared as one-minute blurbs on a TV talk show such as the David Letterman Show or the Oprah Winfrey Show.

- Ask people to imagine a setting in which they would likely share their stories. Have them describe the target audiences. How will that target audience change the way they tell the story?

- Increase the number of stories. When people get good at this, have them try to weave together a series of interconnected stories within a specified time limit.

- Vary the amount of time people have to tell their stories in the middle of the process. For example, start by giving the person three minutes to tell a story; once he or she appears to be in a comfortable "telling" rhythm, flash a sign instructing him or her that there are thirty seconds left to finish the story. Adding time in the middle of a person's telling is another variation.

- Run the activity in pairs with two rounds. Round one: Storytellers have one minute to tell their stories. Ask storytellers to leave the room. Assign listeners one of three roles (very interested in the story they are hearing, neutral, and not interested). Through body language, listeners will project their roles. Without any debriefing, switch roles and go straight into round two. Round two: Ask the new storytellers to leave the room. Instruct listeners to be themselves and to act natural. When the storytellers return to the room, tell them to be sensitive to their listeners to determine the right amount of detail for their stories. Finish round two and do a thorough debriefing. Allow at least thirty to forty-five minutes for this variation.

Tips
- This can be tough for folks, so be lighthearted. Have fun and make sure people do not feel intimidated. Be a cheerleader and not a drill sergeant. Leverage the group as an ally. People will tend to be supportive of one another. Encourage and fuel this kind of energy and feedback. Use the group to help you coach the person.

- Steer people away from getting hung up on figuring out the ideal length for a story. It changes all the time. Expanding and collapsing the story is a mechanical skill that they can hone with deliberate practice. What's harder to master are the observational skills and sensitivity to situational dynamics that are necessary.

- Allow listeners to paraphrase a story.

- If someone becomes stuck or frustrated when telling a story, be ready to jump in with suggestions.

- When you run this activity with people's personal stories, ask them to rate the length of their stories on a scale of 1 to 4, where 1 is very short and 4 is very long. If a story is naturally long, instruct the person to truncate it. For shorter stories, instruct people to expand the amount of detail they share or ask them to piece together two or more stories to increase the effectiveness of their communication.

- Recent stories or ones that are more important to us are easier to expand or collapse than ones that are not.

- Bring in synopses of current movies or books and read them out loud as examples of condensed stories.

- Guide people to look for details in the story that are not critical.

Applications

1. Include this activity in presentation skills workshops.

2. Incorporate this as a skill-building activity during a project team's kickoff meeting. Put in place some practices and standards for sharing stories.

3. Use this activity to mentor leaders. Help them to understand how to leverage their personal and organizational stories in a variety of settings.

Case Study

I was teaching a customer service workshop for a large software and hardware vendor. It was a mix of new customer service representatives and mid-level managers. One woman had just been promoted to manager. She was conscientious, with a penchant for detail. She was known for typing long, detailed histories for every call she took. It was not uncommon for one of her entries to be two pages long. She often worked overtime without punching a clock just to finish logging her calls. During her first thirty days as a new manager, she was drowning in a sea of customer stories and unresolved issues. Each time she spoke with a customer, she could not resist the urge to hear the person's entire history. Then when she went to resolve the customer's issue with shipping, billing, or technical support, she felt compelled to recount the whole story. Other people in the organization dreaded her calls or visits and began to avoid her whenever possible. Needless to say, she was falling hopelessly behind. Throughout the workshop, we did multiple iterations of the Expand and Collapse activity. We started with movies and books and progressed to running the activity with her old customer service logs. With the help of her colleagues, we role played people in shipping, billing, or technical support. She began to see patterns in how she told her stories and what details were less important than others. She gained invaluable feedback from her colleagues, who helped her discover how she could streamline her stories and still be thorough and influential.

Guided Journey

Guided Journey

Background

I've always had a fascination with visualization. As a kid I watched my father read orchestra scores for hours. The studious air of the room could not silence the flurry of sound raging in my father's mind. He did not need an orchestra to enter the music—his mind was a playground full of endless discovery. Later in life, as a competitive fencer, I experienced guided visualization in a more structured manner. Mental rehearsal of motor skills was just the surface. I used guided visualization for planning strategies, fencing imaginary bouts with tough opponents, replaying victories and defeats to look for new insights, and for conditioning cognitive and emotional responses to stressful competitive situations. My formal studies of visualization branched out from sports psychology to an amazing interdisciplinary world rich in techniques, traditions, rituals, and philosophies. I continue to be a student. Through it all, one thing remains. This is a powerful way to use stories to tap into the imagination. What follows here is not even the tip of the iceberg, but it will get you started. It represents some of the ways in which I have been successful in working with guided visualizations in organizations. I encourage you to see this as only the start of a fascinating journey.

Facilitation Level
Difficult

Objectives
1. Engage the imagination to envision new possibilities.
2. Use a collaborative storytelling process to stimulate reflection.
3. Uncover organizational and personal challenges and stimulate creative solutions.

Materials
- Flip chart
- Tape/CD player

Time
Sixty minutes or more

Directions

1. Select a topic or subject for the guided visualization.

2. Facilitate a discussion about desired outcomes for the guided visualization. Keep in mind that the outcomes for the guided visualization will vary from group to group and topic to topic. It's critical that you gain agreement with the group as to what is important to them.

3. Develop a storyboard of the guided visualization with the group. Start by reviewing the outcomes with the group; then ask them to suggest potential scenes and images they associate with these outcomes.

4. Ask people to close their eyes. Run through a breathing and progressive relaxation script. Two samples follow.

> Now I want you to think about the top of your head ... many people don't realize that tension often starts in the little muscles of the scalp, so I want you to think about those little muscles and the skin of your scalp and just allow them to let go and relax ... now all the muscles of your face, just let them go slack ... your forehead and your eyes and eyelids ... the cheeks, mouth, and jaw muscles ... it's a wonderful feeling when you let your face totally relax, because you can actually feel the skin settling, smoothing out ... it might mean that your mouth opens slightly, but whatever's best to you, just let it happen ... unclenching your teeth and relaxing your tongue, because the more you physically relax, the more you can mentally relax ... thinking about your neck and shoulder muscles now, and into the tops of your arms, letting all tensions drain away as you think on down to your elbows ... into your forearms... down through your wrists and into your hands ... right down into the very tips of your fingers and tips of your thumbs ... just letting all those muscles let go and relax ... and now think about your breathing, noticing that you're breathing even more steadily, even more slowly, as you relax more and more, so you can let any tension in the chest area simply drain away as you think on down to your stomach muscles, letting those muscles relax, too ... think down into your back now, the long muscles on either side of the spine, just let those muscles relax, and your waist ... and your main thigh muscles, as you think on down through your knees, down through the shins and calves, just allowing all those areas to relax and let go, as you think on down through your ankles, through your feet, into the very tips of your toes ... all the muscles of your body beautifully relaxed and easy ... very lazy....

Here is another script you can try:

In a moment I'm going to relax you more completely. In a moment I'm going to begin counting backward from 10 to 1.

The moment I say the number 10 you will allow your eyelids to remain closed. The moment I say the number 10, you will, in your mind's eye, see yourself at the top of a small set of stairs.

The moment I say the number 9, and each additional number, you will simply move down those stairs, relaxing more completely. At the base of the stairs is a large feather bed, with a comfortable feather pillow.

The moment I say the number 1 you will simply sink into that bed, resting your head on that feather pillow.

Number 10, eyes closed at the top of those stairs. Ten....

Nine, relaxing and letting go. Nine....

Eight, sinking into a more comfortable, calm, peaceful position....

Seven....

Six...going way down....

Five...moving down those stairs, relaxing more completely....

Four....

Three...breathe in deeply....

Two...On the next number, number 1, simply sinking into that bed, becoming more calm, more peaceful, more relaxed....

One...sinking into that feather bed, let every muscle go limp and loose as you sink into a more calm, peaceful state of relaxation.

5. Go through your guided visualization script. These scripts will include places where you ask people to imagine things and to make decisions; pause after each one to give people time to sit with their images before moving to the next part of the script.

6. When you reach the end of the script, bring people's attention back to the room.

7. Give people a few minutes of silence to process their experience.

8. Debrief the activity.

9. Develop personal or organizational action plans based on the visualization.

Debriefing

- After finishing the guided visualization, people will need a few minutes to process the experience. Do not rush. You will have a range of reactions. People may not want to talk about their experience. Some people may need to trivialize their experience by saying something like, "That's the best sleep I've gotten in days." That's okay. Either all they genuinely got out of the experience was relaxation, which is a good thing unto itself, or they need some time to themselves before they will, if ever, speak about their experience. I have had other people break down in tears. Some people become very analytical and want to dissect every detail of their visualization. Other people become voyeuristic and want to hear other people's experiences before they are willing to talk about their own. There is usually one person in the group who is willing and able to speak about his or her experience in a productive manner that stimulates a positive group discussion. Treat all responses with detached respect, care, and interest. Your job is to validate and gently probe and help the person craft meaning from the experience. Be wary of interjecting too many interpretations of people's experiences.

- Writing helps to clarify the experience. If I have another day with the group, I will ask people to record some of their thoughts. Writing an action plan is also valuable when one of the objectives for the visualization is to change behavior.

- Debrief this activity twice. The first debriefing occurs at the end of the activity. I'll debrief the activity again the following day. Sometimes I give people time before or after the second debriefing to record their thoughts or write action plans.

- *How do guided visualizations facilitate good communication?* All communication begins with our selves. We swim in a sea of thoughts and feelings that toss and turn us in different directions. We are not aware of the forces underneath the surface tugging on our cognition. Guided visualizations give us access to these hidden forces. When we are clear and focused within our selves, our actions and words with others will be more meaningful. Guided visualizations help us morph "internal stories" that are holding us captive in negative ways. We can confront our demons, re-vision our relationships to people, places, and things, and enter deeper realms of our being through the portal of our imaginations.

- *How do you make sense of your experience?* Guided visualizations are like dreams. Time and reflection offer additional insights. Do not look for definitive answers. You are stirring your pot. It's not uncommon to re-encounter people and feelings we have buried or long forgotten. Sorry to be metaphysical here, but this is soul work—there's no telling what you will dredge up. This raw material can be fashioned into anything you want. At its core, guided visualization graces us with opportunities to grow in self-awareness and knowledge. Encourage people to replay their journeys over and over again in their mind's eyes to look for new clues of meaning. By your example, show people it is desirable and beneficial to share the insights they are garnering from their journeys with others. Our learning is always deepened through dialogue with others. Through dialogue we can observe our experiences with new eyes of wonder as we discover how our experiences are interconnected with others.

Variations

- Pre-record the guided visualization if it is a standard one that you plan on using multiple times with no changes to it. It is often easier for people to listen to a recording than to a live voice. For some reason it is less threatening. If possible, include appropriate background music that promotes relaxation.

- Use a script from a book. Here are two books I have found useful:

  The Power of Metaphor by Michael Berman and David Bowman

  Guided Imagery for Groups: Fifty Visualizations That Promote Relaxation, Problem Solving, Creativity, and Well-Being by Andrew E. Schwartz

- Conduct the guided visualization as a discussion. This allows people to do this activity with their eyes open and to leverage each other as learning allies. Skip the progressive relaxation. However, I would suggest asking people to optionally close their eyes for five minutes to relax and get into a reflective state of mind. During this time, play some music. Then ask people to open their eyes and commence with the script, but do it as a discussion.

- Break people into groups of three or four and have them develop their own scripts. This requires a fair amount of time and works best over a several-day period. Be prepared to provide lots of guidance to the groups and be sure to have sample scripts for them to use as a guide. Do this variation in two or three phases, culminating in the guided visualization conducted by the group. The tricky part of this variation is determining how the script will be read when you have multiple groups. I have solved this in a number of different ways—none of which is perfect but each of which has worked with various degrees of success. You can stagger the groups and be the reader for each one. You can have groups take turns being readers for each other. You can ask other facilitators or people not involved in the session to read the script. You can give the group tools for recording their script. You can collect the scripts ahead of time and make a recording for each group. For this, I recommend digitally recording the script to your laptop and either burning a CD or copying the file to a memory stick that can be used in one of the participant's laptops. Sometimes there are people in the group who helped develop the script but who are not interested in doing the guided visualization. This is the least desirable option.

- Develop the script, but let people do the guided visualization on their own. This works well for offsite, multi-day retreats. I usually pair this option with a journaling activity that participants do as part of the assignment and that we then debrief the next day.

- For group interventions when the guided visualization is being used to help people see and appreciate each other's perspectives, keep a running log of significant stories people share with the group. You can use Story Collaging™ to quickly create a list of stories. Decide collaboratively which stories you want to use in a script—or if pressed for time you can decide without the group's input. Build a script with the situations and people found in these stories.

- Have people record their thoughts in a stream of consciousness journal as you read the script. Although this is not as effective, people's imaginations will still be engaged. With light music in the background, silent pauses, and the right atmosphere, this is a safe way to help people reflect.

Tips

- Prepare people for this activity by leading a discussion on imagery and visualization. Sports psychology is a good place to start. It's imperative that people feel safe. If someone has never done a guided visualization, he or she will have lots of concerns. People need to understand that you are not hypnotizing them. Without trust this activity cannot and will not work.

- Whatever the level of trust is between yourself and the group, not everyone will be comfortable doing this activity. Give people the freedom to opt out of the activity without any pressure from you or the rest of the group.

- Do not abuse the trust and power being given to you by the group. You are inducing alpha and theta brain waves in people. People are very susceptible to suggestions in this state. It is the same state of consciousness induced by trained hypnotists and coercive brainwashers.

- Approach this activity with humility and minimize the didactic material in your script. Place people in a scene and then let them simulate their own internal representations and behaviors. Let their mind's eyes draw the pictures, not you. Provide just enough detail to stimulate their imaginations. For example, if I wanted people to imagine a difficult meeting. . .

  You are leaving your office to go the meeting, what are you bringing with you…[pause to let them imagine]

  As you walk toward the meeting, who do you see in the hallway? Are you saying anything to this person? What is this person saying to you?

Pause for a moment before you enter the room where the meeting will take place. Who do you see in the room? Where is this person sitting? Who is this person talking to? What is this person saying?

- Develop the script with lots of collaborative input. This reduces people's apprehensions about the process and gives them greater control over their experience. If you do not develop the script with participants, explain in enough detail what they will be going through. Even if you do not collaboratively develop the script, get the group's agreement on the objectives for the guided visualization. They need to now why they are doing it and what outcomes are expected.

- Be mindful of how you use your voice. It should be soft, gentle, quiet, but firm. Read each word with care and meaning. You need to live your script as you read it to the group. People are relying on your voice to transport their imaginations. You cannot be mechanical or distracted. If there isn't a clock with a second hand in the room, keep a timing device by your side. When you give people instructions to imagine something, give them at least thirty seconds and up to three minutes. How much time you allot for each pause depends on the complexity of what you are asking them to imagine and how many other places in the script you need to pause. If you are limited by time, adjust your script with fewer places where you pause to allow people to imagine things—do not try to do all of them by shortening the length of the pause. This will disrupt people's relaxed state and not give them enough time to generate rich imagery and feelings.

- Ask people to turn off cell phones or any other devices that make sounds or vibrate. Encourage people to get comfortable. In some settings, I have let people lie down on the floor or take off their shoes. Use your judgment as to what is appropriate or practical given the venue and circumstances.

Applications

1. When a group becomes stuck, use guided visualizations as a way of stimulating creative thinking and idea generation.

2. Incorporate guided visualization during strategic planning retreats.

3. Use guided visualization with change management steering groups to help them imagine the impact of the proposed change on all the stakeholders.

4. Add guided visualization to any type of workshop during which you want to encourage stress management, personal growth, or reflection.

Case Study

I was teaching a two-day time management workshop and struggling with the materials. People at the organization had been through two rounds of layoffs. In an effort to increase productivity, management had mandated all middle managers of one of the divisions to attend the time management workshop. People were supposed to learn how to be more effective with their time and discover new secrets to motivating their direct reports to be more efficient.

We all went through the charade of marching through the materials. I put on my best upbeat trainer face and led the troops through a series of behavioral rat mazes aimed at reconditioning their bad habits. People had no problems with the mechanics of time management. I knew in my heart of hearts that people did not need any more tools, strategies, or best practices. What they wanted was a way to cope with their frustration, anger, and feelings of being overwhelmed by all of the work being demanded of them now. At the start of the second day, I decided to toss the materials.

While solving the larger organizational issues of change and corporate culture were beyond the scope of my role, I decided to take an indirect route to address people's anxieties. Nothing in the course dealt with work/life balance. I believed that if I could help people envision a healthy balance between their work and personal lives I might be able to help them neutralize some of the negative energy they were feeling about their jobs. I didn't want them to feel enslaved by their jobs. Nor did I want them to clinically separate their personal lives from their work lives. The two are interconnected. Why endure eight hours of torture a day?

After explaining the mechanics of guided visualization, we talked about what they wanted to get out of the experience. Two people out of twenty-four did not feel comfortable doing the activity, so I let them opt out without any pressure. Using the list of things the group wanted out of their lives and work, I improvised an easy script. After ten minutes of progressive relaxation, I asked them to imagine one of their favorite places. Then we walked through six scenes that represented different aspects of their personal and work lives (e.g., time with family, friends, community, interacting with colleagues at work). For each scene, I provided a short description followed by a series of questions. After each set of questions, I paused for three minutes to let them put their imaginations to work. When we finished the script, I brought people's attention back to the room and asked them to open their eyes when they were ready. I let people sit in silence for five minutes before debriefing the activity. Without any hesitation, people started sharing their visions. People were moved by their visions and even more moved by the group's discussions. They began to articulate new possibilities their visions had offered them to counter-balance the negative period they were experiencing at work. One man described in vivid emotional detail the joys of rolling in the grass tickling his children. The two people who had opted out of the activity were amazed by the experiences of their colleagues. They asked me for a copy of the script so that they could have someone at home walk them through it.

Listening As an Ally™

Listening As an Ally™

A Repetitive Question Activity
Shared by Barry Rosen, Interaction Associates

Background

Many years ago, I attended a three-day leadership workshop in San Francisco. One afternoon's topic was of particular interest to me—how our fondly held beliefs about "the way things are" limit our ability to have the kind of impact we want in our work and lives. There were 200+ participants in the session and two workshop leaders; I'll call them Bob and Julio to protect their confidentiality. About thirty minutes into the session, several of the participants were getting restless. The main presenter (Bob) was laboring—however earnestly—with his explanation of the basic model. Predictably, one participant after another began raising objections and concerns. It appeared to me that many people were experiencing growing anxiety. Will Bob recover? Is this session getting out of control? Should I say something? Should I tell others to just relax and let Bob finish? What should I think? What should I do?

What occurred next in the room was quite extraordinary. In the midst of the growing chaos, Julio walked onto the stage and said, "May I have your attention?" The hubbub subsided to a murmur and the murmur to silence.

"Shortly, I'm going to make a request of you. I imagine many of you have developed some very interesting—and perhaps accurate—opinions about what's going on here. Some of you may be disturbed, disappointed, and even angry with Bob or other members of this group. Whatever the case, I'm going to ask you now to try something. *For the next twenty minutes, listen to Bob as if he were the protagonist in a great novel. Simply listen to him as you would listen to the hero of a dramatic story.* Is there anyone not willing to try this simple experiment?"

No one raised his hand. A collective deep breath followed. Julio left the stage and Bob returned to his presentation. Bob repeated much of what he had already said, in much the same way as he had spoken before. He spoke for another forty-five minutes.

At the end-of-day evaluation, the overwhelming feedback was that Bob's presentation—and the re-framed relationship to Bob—was the most meaningful experience of the workshop so far.

A few years later—and after many hundreds of failed and successful practice opportunities—I coined the phrase "Listening As an Ally" to represent the kind of

listening that holds the speaker as the protagonist of a great human story still un-
folding.

Facilitation Level
Moderate

Objectives
1. Experience listening to someone's story without rendering judgment.
2. Expand your ability to provide the support a speaker might need to express
   him/herself fully, honestly, and authentically.
3. Generate compassion for yourself (as listener) and the speaker.

Materials
- Flip chart or prepared overhead or PowerPoint slide (see Step 1)

Time
Thirty to forty-five minutes

Directions
1. Select a topical question that will have meaning to the group, e.g., "What do
   you think or feel about the impending organization change?" Write the question on a flip chart (or PPT slide) so that everyone in the room can see it.
2. Ask the group to divide into pairs, and assign themselves as Person A and
   Person B.
3. Tell the group that the Bs will be the first listeners. As listeners, their job is to
   ask their partners the question. After their partners respond, the listeners simply say, "Thank you," and then repeat the question. This process continues for
   three to five minutes.
4. The speaker, Person A, should answer the question each time as if the question
   is being asked for the first time. She should answer the questions with a word,
   a phrase, or a short sentence. She should not explain the statement. She should
   aim to survey her feelings and thoughts and express as much as possible
   about the topic. It's okay for the speaker to repeat him/herself.
5. After the prescribed time, the workshop leader asks the pairs to thank each
   other and to switch roles. The process then repeats.
6. Debrief the exercise.

Debriefing

- The power of this activity lies in its simplicity. There is no need to make "deep meaning" points afterward. The participants will come up with some great material themselves. As the trainer, you might try simply saying "thank you," as with the activity itself.

- *What insights or feelings did you have as you spoke about your experience? What insights or feelings did you have as you listened to your partner?* Simply "receiving" another's words without comment provides the "space" for the other to explore and reveal feelings and ideas that have meaning and importance. Curiosity and empathy establish the pathway to appreciation and compassion for another human being's experience. By simply asking, "What do you feel and think about. . .?" we can engage our curiosity. By viewing the listener as the "hero of the story," we can engage our compassion.

- *How might you apply what you've learned immediately? To the work we are doing here together? At work in general? In other aspects of your life?* When we have something on our minds, most of us simply want someone to witness and pay attention to us while we speak about it. That's the first step to an authentic connection. Listening as an "ally" is listening with the intent to receive, understand, appreciate, and have compassion for the speaker. It takes a conscious choice on the listener's part to move beyond immediate reactions and assessments (e.g., listening as a judge or adversary) to listen as an ally.

Variations

- Conduct the activity with trios instead of pairs. The third person observes the other two speaking and listening. Example of flow: B listens to A. C listens to B. A listens to C.

- Instead of using the question format: "What do you think or feel about. . . ?" substitute: "What do think I feel or think about. . .?" At the end of each round, the listener briefly (one to two minutes) confirms and/or refines the speaker's perceptions of the listener's experience.

Tips

- When listening to the speaker, the listener should refrain from making extensive gestures—physical or verbal. The listener should instead use subtle, supportive gestures, such as a gentle smile or murmur.

- The pairs or trios should try to refrain from laughing or kidding about the activity "because it's kind of different." This behavior will undermine the impact of the experience for both (or all) parties.

- The activity is not a contest about how many things the speaker can say in three minutes. The speaker should take his or her time—breathing and reflecting after each "share."

Applications

1. If you facilitate meetings, you can use this activity to evaluate the meeting using the topic: "What did you feel or think about this meeting?"

2. In coaching sessions (as coach), you can apply the repetitive question technique to elicit content before exploring the coachee's experience in more detail.

3. As a journaling activity, you can ask yourself the repetitive question.

Case Study

A large Petrochemicals company was engaged in a Six Sigma quality effort to improve efficiencies and catalyze innovation. The senior managers of two plant sites—located within twenty miles of each other—decided to merge the plant management teams and coordinate production across sites. The decision was supported by senior managers at both sites, particularly in light of the impending retirements of five of the twelve managers, including one of the plant managers.

Bob G. became the plant manager of the combined site structure.

The change would require a shift in several management assignments, as well as the direct reporting structure at the mid-management and supervision levels.

Bob had worked tirelessly over the previous three months to guide the decision-making process. While the change guaranteed no job losses at either site (except for normal attrition), many supervisors and line personnel were fearful about the change. Through the grapevine, Bob heard a few stories about grumbling and criticism.

Bob took the stories personally. At a day-long meeting of supervisors and mid-managers, he challenged all attendees to speak to him directly about their concerns and stop fueling the discontent with "rumors and speculation."

One supervisor, Carl, raised his hand and asked: "How will the reorganization affect specific job assignments?"

Bob snapped back: "I don't have all the answers! Do you guys expect me to handle everything?"

Carl responded calmly: "Bob, I know you're trying to make this work for all of us. I don't expect you to have all the answers; I just want to know what you're thinking."

Bob was startled by Carl's clear and reasonable statement. He felt embarrassed for jumping to conclusions. Bob realized he had been "listening as an adversary"—believing his mid-managers were ganging up on him, and lashing out based in

Listening As an Ally™   **107**

reaction to an untested belief. In fact, he really didn't know what people were thinking.

At that strategic moment, Bob made a conscious choice. Bob chose to acknowledge his misstep and to "listen as an ally."

Bob said: "I regret my reaction to your question, Carl. Your question is perfectly reasonable. I also appreciate your mentioning my effort to make this work for everyone. But you know, I'm realizing I can't do that well without hearing your questions and concerns. If I don't have the answers, we can work together to figure things out. How does that sound?"

A noticeable ease of tension occurred throughout the room. With help from one of the supervisors, Bob facilitated a brainstorming session of questions and concerns, asking questions along the way to clarify and validate specific items.

Bob felt the load of responsibility release from his shoulders. Listening with the intention to really understand made it so much easier for him than listening with the intention to defend or control.

I was at Bob's meeting that day. Toward the end of the session, before action planning and the meeting evaluation, Bob asked me for my observations. I commented on the shift that occurred earlier in the meeting and acknowledged everyone for "listening as an ally." I asked the group and Bob if I they might be interested in doing a twenty-minute exercise to prepare them for making "next step commitments." They agreed. I then facilitated the "repetitive response" exercise described above to the question: "What do you feel or think about the meeting today?"

The impact on the group was profound. In the meeting evaluation, participants commented that the exercise helped:

- Deepen their appreciation of their own and others' experience of the change effort
- Generate new ideas for implementing the reorganization
- Remind them of their own responsibility in being compassionate leaders in their own functional areas

The Magic Three

The Magic Three

Background

I've always been a fan of the number 3 and one day it came to my rescue. I was filling in as a facilitator for a colleague of mine. It was early in my career and, not being familiar with the workshop's materials, I was at a loss as to what to do with the group. There were two hours left on the clock and we were ready to go into the workshop's last exercise, which was supposed to last ten minutes. I began to panic. My colleague had warned me not to end the session early. I decided to ad lib and modify the directions of the exercise. The exercise called for participants to share with partners an experience from their past that would be different today if they applied the communication principles we had learned during the course. I put people into groups of four and instructed them to share three experiences instead of one. Something very unexpected and magical happened; and since then the Magic Three has never disappointed me.

Facilitation Level
Easy

Objectives
1. Provide a structured activity to guide people through an experience of reflection.
2. Practice authentic communication.
3. Create a connection with listeners.

Materials
- None

Time
Up to fifteen minutes per person

Directions
1. Give this as an overnight assignment during a multi-day workshop or retreat.
2. Tell participants to think of three personal stories that have some relationship among them.

3. Ask participants to share their stories with the group the next day.

4. Debrief the activity.

Debriefing

- *The good news:* this is *almost always* an easy activity to debrief given the richness of the experience for the teller and the group listening to him or her. The activity runs itself. Your main job is to give people ample time to react to the story. When a teller is finished, it is a good idea to allow some silence in the room. Start the debriefing process with the teller. Ask him, "How did that feel?" Alternatively, if he hasn't done so already ask him to explain how he came up with the three stories. If it was an emotionally charged set of stories, feel free to ask a few follow-on questions about one or more of the stories. However, be prepared to redirect the group if one or more people become too engrossed in the details of a story or pursue tangential lines of questioning. Some of this sort of thing is okay but can quickly take a group off track.

- Next, if it hasn't started happening naturally already, ask the group to provide feedback, impressions, and reactions to the teller. Some people may even feel compelled to spontaneously share a story of their own. Encourage the teller and then the group to reflect on the relationship between the stories and discuss insights that have emerged from them.

- Tie the outcomes of the activity to the major themes, lessons, and insights of the workshop.

- *How did the teller's communication style change when he or she was telling a story? How were you impacted as a listener?* People who find it difficult to speak in front of a group will experience a real connection with their audience. Likewise, listeners will describe the teller as engaging, and the stories as rich or stimulating. This is the result of the teller reliving her experience.

- *What's the connection between the stories? How and why did these three stories become associated with one another?* Before participating in this activity someone may have never associated these stories to one another. In some cases, this may be the first time he or she is suddenly recalling an experience from the past that was forgotten. One story leads to the trail of another. This is the reflective power of stories. Stories by their nature are multi-threaded. Frays of the thread can twist and unwind in lots of unexpected ways. As stories come apart, they can be rejoined to others to form new networks of meaning and significance.

Variations

- Vary the number of stories (however, it should be two at a minimum and under most circumstances not more than five).

- Have participants work on the assignment during the workshop.
- Tell stories during a working lunch.
- Change the type of stories you ask participants to think about and tell (e.g., from personal ones to work-related ones). Depending on the nature of the workshop and the composition of your group, you can be very specific in the parameters you set.
- Limit the number of participants in the activity.
- Spread out the number of people who share their stories across multiple days.
- Break participants into smaller groups and have people share their stories within the smaller groups. Ask each group to select one of its members' stories and have a member of the group other than the owner of the story retell it to the group at large.
- Invite one of the participants to facilitate the group debriefing.
- Ask everyone to anonymously write down three major things that struck them about the stories (do this before any group debriefing). Provide the feedback to the story owner.
- Add a visual component to the activity. Instruct participants to create a collage or some other kind of visual to document their stories.
- Encourage listeners to share any of their stories that have been triggered by another person's stories.

Tips

- Be purposefully vague in your instructions. This is one of those times when less is more. Some participants may struggle with the directions. Encourage them to grapple with the ambiguity. Out of the ambiguity comes the reflective soul-searching that is necessary. Be aware that detail-oriented people may become slightly frustrated by your lack of clear and precise directions. That's okay. Apologize to them and explain that it will make more sense to them after the activity. Realize that you may need to bear the brunt of their temporary aggravation. At this point there is no need to relieve it. It would only alleviate your feelings, but not help the participant. Afterward, point out that the success of the activity is contingent on participants' finding a path through their experiences. I'll sometimes joke and say, "In the words of Hamlet, 'I must be cruel to be kind.'"
- Emphasize that stories need to have some sort of thread or connection between them. Encourage participants to look for non-linear connections. That is to say, the stories they select that have a relationship to each other can be from very different times and parts of their lives.

- Do not provide your own example in advance. After one or more participants share their three stories, you may feel free to share yours. The purpose in doing so is to generate greater trust, intimacy, and authenticity with the group. Your stories as a facilitator of the group may also be a good tool for defusing any intense or difficult dynamics that arise in the group as a result of someone else's stories.
- Never judge the stories or anyone's response/reaction to them.
- Allow there to be some silence after a participant shares his or her three stories.
- Insist that people come to the front of the room to tell their stories. Unless someone is completely emotionally or physically incapable of being in front of the room, it is an essential part of the activity. People overcome their inhibitions about speaking when they tell stories.
- Confiscate notes from the participant sharing his or her stories. Despite whatever inclination he or she may have, he or she will not need notes, and using them will prevent the person from reliving his or her story.
- Limit the number of tellers if you are pressed for time. People listening learn from the activity sometimes as much if not more than tellers.

Applications
1. This is a great activity to use in any offsite retreat.
2. Incorporate this as a team-building activity or let members of a team take turns sharing their magic three at the start of regular meetings.
3. Use as an icebreaker or lunch activity during an event.

Case Study

I was facilitating a workshop on personal effectiveness in business. Len was a no-nonsense technology project manager for a nuclear research company. Len possessed exceptional communication skills. He was clear, precise, succinct, and very articulate. However, despite his technical prowess as a communicator, Len observed that he often failed to connect with people on an emotional level.

I gave Len two assignments. The first assignment was to take a complex newspaper article on a controversial topic and in thirty seconds or less provide a summary of the article's information and make a recommendation. Len's second assignment was the *Magic Three.*

Len performed the newspaper activity with the prowess of a polished politician. He was absolutely brilliant. I wanted him to serve as an example of how to deliver an effective executive sound bite. There are many times when we have thirty seconds or less to make an elevator pitch.

After appropriate accolades, I asked Len to share his three stories with us. In a matter of a few seconds, Len's body language began to transform in front of our very eyes. His erect, formal stature was replaced with a more relaxed posture. As he began to share his stories with the group, he moved to the edge of a table to sit down. Here is a recapitulation of his stories as I remember them:

> I've always been a fairly private person so joining groups was never high on my list of things to do. About seven years ago I decided to get more involved with my local Catholic church group. I was surprised at how quickly I began forming a core group of friends who became a central part of my life. Weekends were filled with fishing trips, barbecues with our wives and families, and general fraternizing with my new cohorts. It had been a long time since I had experienced this kind of camaraderie and I was relishing every minute of it. As a group, we kept growing closer and closer. Even my family was caught off guard by the quality and depth of relationships I developed with a bunch of total strangers. This continued for several years. After a horrible car accident, I found myself in the hospital recovering from a life-threatening back surgery and long days of excruciating pain blunted by the constant dripping of numbing morphine. Everything was a haze. I was in a complete fog of pain, depression, and despair. During these horrific weeks, there were two pins of light that got me through these dark times, my family and my friends. Family you kind of expect to be there for you, but I was amazed at the dedication and energy my friends gave to me when I needed them the most. To this day I believe my friends were a special gift granted to me to ensure I pulled through a very trying experience. A couple of years later my buddies wanted to go on a weekend retreat with the church. I resisted, but after a lot of cajoling I agreed to go. We had a fantastic time, and the retreat was filled with lots of soulful opportunities to recharge our batteries and put the challenges of life into perspective. My friends made the retreat a special experience and I returned home with fresh vigor and zest. A day after my return, my father died unexpectedly. I believe my friends and the retreat were granted to me as a form of preparation for my father's death. I was able to be a source of comfort and strength for my family. I had more emotional energy to give to them. To this day, I am eternally grateful for friendship and all of the richness it has given me in life.

Unfortunately, my retelling is pale in comparison to Len's original account. It's missing all of the other subtle forms of communication that accompanied it, such as body language, eye contact, and tone of voice. When Len finished, there was silence in the room. People needed a moment to exit their imaginations and reenter the workshop's frame of reference. Ken confessed he had never told these stories to anyone else before; and prior to the workshop he never would have dreamed of sharing them in a work environment. He reflected on the powerful connection of friendship he discovered in the three stories. Then Ken made an amazing leap of insight. He concluded that he needed to be selectively more vulnerable with people at work in order to improve his personal effectiveness. Ken committed to spending more time cultivating relationships in his organization. Stories, he discovered, are one of the best tools for building effective, meaningful relationships.

Mirror

Mirror

Background

I was having a heck of time helping a client streamline its help desk processes. There was a lot of resistance to imagining any changes. The support group had spent a lot of money on a web-based tool for tracking and resolving trouble tickets. The issue, of course, was not the tool, but I had an idea. I pulled the director of the group aside and asked him to give me an hour and a half with his team. After a little cajoling, he agreed. I went through the trouble ticket database and selected five recent tickets. Next, I invited the internal customers who had submitted the tickets to meet with us and share their stories with the group. The day arrived for the meeting and people had no idea what we were going to do. After warming the group up and getting them relaxed, I informed them that we were going to review the five recent trouble ticket stories from two perspectives. First from the customer and then from the engineers who had been responsible for resolving it. In order to facilitate open communication, I asked the engineer associated with the ticket being discussed to leave the room. Likewise, I asked each customer to leave the room when the engineers shared their stories. As to be expected, there was some defensive face saving, but the stories yielded lots of rich information. The group was able to shift its thinking and see new opportunities for improving its processes. And customers got a chance to understand what goes on behind the scenes and give their thoughts, ideas, and suggestions. After a very successful meeting, I resolved to tweak this process and use it in different settings.

Facilitation Level
Moderate

Objectives
1. Use stories to communicate multiple perspectives.
2. Practice entering other people's frames of reference to understand multiple perspectives.
3. Generate out-of-the-box thinking that takes into account multiple perspectives.

Materials
- Flip chart and markers

Time
Forty-five to sixty minutes

Directions
1. Take two to three minutes and generate a list of contentious topics with the group (i.e., current affairs, politics, etc.).

2. Vote for a topic.

3. Ask for two volunteers to act as speakers for each side of the topic.

4. Before listening to the speakers, have the rest of the group write down which side of the issue they are on. Collect the votes, which you will tally later.

5. Give each speaker up to five minutes to present his or her views. Alternate speakers representing different sides of the topic. It's critical that people present their viewpoints with a collection of stories. None of the speakers is allowed to hear another, so send them out of the room until it is their turn. The rest of the group is allowed only to listen.

6. After all the speakers have had a turn, have them stand in front of the room on opposite sides.

7. Instruct the rest of the group to go stand on the side of the room that represents their viewpoint.

8. Tally the votes from the beginning of the activity. Explore whether anyone changed his or her view as result of listening to the speakers.

9. Facilitate a ten-to-fifteen-minute discussion in which people on opposing sides must demonstrate that they understand the other side's perspective.

10. Let everyone sit down. Debrief the activity.

Debriefing
- You want to see a shift in people's imaginations. Parroting the details of another person's perspective is an excellent critical thinking skill, but we're after more with this activity. Are people trying to feel, know, and project themselves into perspectives that run contrary to their own? Some people will only get the mechanics of this critical communication practice. In other people, you will detect a new appreciation for opposing views. While they may not change their views, they will develop a softer perspective that prepares them to enter into a dialogue with others during which they will be open to collaboratively discovering new possibilities.

- People will feel invigorated by talking about difficult and contentious topics. We avoid these conversations because we believe they are danger zones. People like the freedom to speak about these topics, especially in a work environment in which these topics are taboo. In rare circumstances, you may end up playing referee. The format of the activity and the group dynamics it produces usually prevent people from getting out of hand or insulting each other, but you need to be watchful. Once you set this activity in motion, people really enjoy it and want it to work. They keep each other in check while they simultaneously give each other permission to be true to their thoughts, feelings, and experiences. Developing the skills to enter into meaningful discussion requires that we be willing and able to enter new frames of references.

- *Why do stories communicate perspectives more effectively?* Stories contain our experiences. Listening to someone's experience does not challenge our cherished views in the same way that other forms of discourse can. A speaker invites us to imagine his or her experience. Agreement and disagreement fade from view. Our focus moves to a new mental space. We enter a frame of reference that functions as a window looking out onto a view filled with new data for us to vicariously consider. We are more receptive to stories, possibly because, whether we know it consciously or not, we have a wealth of them. We recognize that we have different experiences and that these experiences have a profound effect on how we see the world.

- *What communication advantage do we gain when we can quickly and easily enter new frames of reference?* Oftentimes we do not have the advantage of hearing people's stories. We need to be able to imagine their perspectives. Constructing frames of references is an act of imagination. We tell ourselves a story. Not just one, but many stories. The more stories we consider, the more flexible we will be in our communication with others. Our interactions are no longer stagnant and based on rigid perceptions. Our words and actions become more fluid. We actively probe and adjust our tack as we gain more information and confidence of our understanding of someone else's perspective. Our ultimate goal in communication is to connect with others. It's a great pleasure to experience the world from other people's perspectives. It is enriching, humbling, and deepening. Developing the capacity to enter frames of references radically changes the nature of communication and will make us feel more alive and less alone.

- *How do stories and entering new frames of references promote out-of-the-box thinking?* Stories and frames of references are another way of understanding active listening. When people feel heard, and when they have an opportunity to share their perspectives in a way that is compelling and that enables you to demonstrate that you have appreciated their perspectives by involving our hearts and minds, they become open to hearing our perspectives. It becomes possible to find common ground and move toward creatively resolving tensions that have gotten in the way of finding solutions. Using stories to construct and move through frames of references creates patterns of meaning. It gets our creative juices going. It promotes collaboration without sacrificing individualism.

Variations

- Use an editorial column from a newspaper or magazine.

- Have people write down a recent annoying experience (e.g., bad customer service). Break people into small groups and have them share their stories. Instruct each group to try to imagine the perspective of the other person/ people in the story.

- Use an organizational policy that many people dislike.

Tips

- This is an important activity to frame well in the beginning. Be clear that you are challenging people to entertain a perspective different from their own. Agreeing or disagreeing with the perspectives being shared is peripheral to the activity.

- Another key aspect of this activity is showing people that when they lack information they can still generate plausible stories to explore someone else's perspective. Stories enable this kind of creative thinking.

- If you generate a list of topics, keep the group focused. Ask people to refrain from getting embroiled in a discussion.

- When discussing the issue, do not take sides. Your job is to remain neutral. You do not want to sway the dynamics of the group. It's important that you do not misuse your positional power as the facilitator.

- You'll have to provide some examples and guidance for people. Help people to reflect on their past experiences or stories they have heard from others. This is at the heart of this activity. Let speakers know you will stop them if they become too dependent on statistics and didactic explanations to justify their viewpoints. This is not a debate. You may want to take a short break before beginning this activity to give speakers a chance to organize their thoughts. Spend a little time with each speaker and make sure they have some stories to share. Provide speakers with some story prompts. For example, what experiences have contributed to you forming this viewpoint? Do you remember any of the stories you have read or heard that have influenced you?

- Listeners are not allowed to ask any questions. If you feel its necessary, you can give people a chance to ask questions when all the speakers are done. Be careful; questions can turn into a debate. Be prepared to stop it if one gets started. When I have time, I'll give people a chance to write down their questions and give them to me. Then I act as a moderator by reading the questions and directing each one to one of the speakers to respond.

- Don't be surprised if some people switch from their original positions. Take the time to explore what caused them to change their minds. Be gentle. If someone changes his or her mind, he or she may still feel tenuous about the decision. Your or the group's inquiries should not cause the person to become insecure. Explain that you are interested in understanding the process he or she went through in reaching the new position.

Applications

1. Incorporate this activity into customer service training programs. Run through the activity and then repeat a variation of it using customer service stories.

2. Use this activity to help salespeople learn how to enter a customer's frame of reference to anticipate and appreciate a customer's needs, concerns, and questions.

3. Customize a version of this activity process as an intervention and communication tool for people who are going through change management events involving mergers, acquisitions, or any reorganization initiatives.

Case Study

I was in New York getting ready to kick off a week of executive coaching with a team of senior managers from various functional areas. One of the strong themes that emerged during the needs analysis phase of my intervention was the team's lack of appreciation for each other's organizational needs and objectives. Everyone reported frustration with the amount of energy they needed to expend in order to safeguard their priorities and agendas. I assembled the group for a half-day session and ran the activity with a provocative editorial about whether people should have to undergo random security checks on the subway. This was a vocal group, so I had no trouble finding two volunteers to represent each side of the issue. I had everyone record his or her initial opinions. I gave the group a five-minute stretch break while I tallied the votes and made sure the speakers were ready to share their perspectives through stories. Then I sent one of the speakers out of the room. I gave each speaker three minutes to pitch his views. The first speaker told a story of the great sacrifice and hardship his son was enduring overseas to protect the United States. He said he wanted to be an urban soldier and step up to the plate to do his part, even if it meant a minor inconvenience of being searched. Then he asked us if we were willing to join him. The second speaker began by telling us about his father's cursed existence in a censored society and how his father was so proud of the freedom and rights he found in the United States. He described how his father instilled in him a passion to protect those rights. Before listening to the speakers, 40 percent were against random security searches on the subway. By the time we were done, the group was evenly split in its opinion and everyone had a new perspective derived from compelling personal stories. While there were still differences, each side saw that the other side cared about many of the same things. Each group had very personal reasons for believing their approach and conclusion was the best. Then we discussed the link between the activity and their cross functional communication challenges. The group agreed that they did not take enough time to understand each other's perspectives. They also agreed to become more aware of the stories influencing their perspectives and to share them with each other. Great in principle, but I had a lot of work ahead of me to help equip managers with the communication competencies that they needed to realize the benefits of their insights.

Random Conversation

Random Conversation

Background

One morning I was sitting at a table with a group of participants eating breakfast and chatting. One guy who was flipping through a newspaper started reading an article out loud to us. We just sat there and listened. About a quarter of the way through the article, someone began to share a personal experience triggered by the article. Then another person did the same. I was struck by how easy it is for people to tell stories when they are relaxed and when there is a good stimulus. I decided to try to re-create this phenomenon in this activity.

Facilitation Level
Moderate

Objectives
1. Help people experience how stories can be triggered by any stimuli.
2. Practice selecting relevant experiences to share when communicating.
3. Develop the ability to scan new information and find personal connections.

Materials
- Newspaper or magazine article

Time
Fifteen to twenty minutes

Directions
1. Clip out a newspaper or magazine article on any subject.
2. Read the article out loud to the group.
3. Invite listeners to respond with stories.

Debriefing
- Be sure to differentiate between commentaries and stories. Most of the stories shared should be of a personal nature. If people are spouting off their opinions without sharing an experience, even if it's someone else's experience, then

they are not practicing storytelling. Gently point out the difference. Be patient. People will not have a clear understanding of the difference between the two. Often one bleeds into the other. If people share a short story and then follow up with some commentary, that's okay. Just don't let them go on for too long. Stories keep people in the realm of listening and imagination, whereas commentaries are more left-brained. The danger with this is that people get trapped in being critical and lose the reflective learning inherent in stories.

- *How does the listening process change when you look for stories?* We process information differently when we look for relationships between what we hear and our experiences. Passive listening becomes active listening; we become more invested in what is being communicated. There is a danger of becoming derailed in our minds by the tangents stimulated by our stories. In other words, what starts out as active listening can become passive listening again if we cannot quickly redirect our attention to the communicator. The trick is to become conscious of the stories that anchor our relationships to the information being shared and then gently refocus our attention on the speaker.

- *What is the nature of the connection between your story and the article?* When we work with stories, we discover the expansive nature of our minds. The connection between the story and the article may not be a very direct one. It can be very loosely related. We are accustomed to organizing information into hierarchies and clear, concrete taxonomies, but our minds do not always work in the same way. Stories allow us to move through associations in non-linear and surprising ways. With stories, the permanency of the connections is not critical. We are constantly engaged in regrouping and associating what we are experiencing in the moment with what we have experienced in the past and with our assumptions about the future.

- *How effective is one story in stimulating others?* One story usually leads to another. Even if a story doesn't lead to another one right away, it might the next time we revisit it. This happens even if we are not involved in doing this on a conscious level; our minds replay our stories and treat them as precious jigsaw pieces of a never-ending puzzle. Stories work best in chains of cross-referenced experiences. Working with stories opens a flood gate of nuances and nooks and crannies. These can be explored in conversation with another person or in a reflective process with ourselves.

Variations
- This activity can be done in pairs or small groups.
- Tell people to bring in an article of their choice. It's essential they select an article that is important to them. Have people read their articles out loud and then

let people respond with stories. After the listener responds, ask the reader to share a story. Then spend a few minutes exploring the relationship between the stories and the article.

- Use an article with lots of pictures. Show only the pictures of the article. Have people jot down stories triggered by the pictures. Then read the article. Have people jot down stories triggered by the text of the article. Compare the stories.

- Instruct the listeners to say "pause" every time they think of a story. Have them jot down short descriptions of their stories. When they have finished making their notes, instruct them to say "continue." Encourage people to record as many stories as they can.

- Vary the amount of time given to reading the article. Try very short sound bites of one to three minutes. The activity will yield different effects with long readings that are in the range of ten minutes.

- Hand out a stack of newspaper and magazines. Give people ten minutes to select articles. Ask them to record on index cards the reasons why they selected the articles they did. If it's because time was running out and they did not know what to select that's fine, but usually people will have some reason. Have people pair off. Each person gives his or her partner the article selected, and the partner then reads it out loud. Afterward the listener (the person who originally selected the article) responds with his or her stories. Ask them to describe any relationship they see between what they wrote on their index cards and the stories they shared. Then give the readers the opportunity to comment on any relationships they see between the two. When finished, switch roles.

Tips
- Humor is a good way to introduce and demo this activity. I like using cartoons such as Gary Larson's *The Far Side* or Charles Schultz's *Peanuts.* The cartoons get people's juices going and encourage them to laugh and relax. There is usually someone in a group with a good sense of humor who will have a quick, short story to tell triggered by the cartoon. Another strategy I have used to warm people up to this activity is to talk about a current event or recent newspaper article at the beginning of a session or after a break. In the process of doing so, I will share a personal story and then without any huge fanfare or lengthy explanation I will conversationally invite people to share their stories triggered by the article. When I introduce the activity later in the session, I ask people to remember our discussion earlier in the day. This helps to create an experiential anchor for people to have an idea of how the activity works.

- Varying the amount of reading time allows you to emphasize different kinds of learning experiences. Shorter reading times of one to three minutes in length challenge listeners to find relevant stories quickly. It develops people's awareness of how stories can be triggered by almost any stimuli at any time. Longer reading times during which listeners keep a running record of stories promotes reflection. It encourages people to find more stories and look for the connections between them.

- For people struggling to come up with a story, guide them to share any associations they have with the information in the article. You want people to be sensitive to how things are interrelated with one another. Maybe it's an item from a news broadcast or an opinion they overheard someone else share. Once you've gone this far, see whether, with a little more probing, this enables you to elicit a story. If the person finds one, be sure to point it out and celebrate it. For extremely difficult cases, goad people to react to the article by giving their opinions. Without lingering on their opinions or reactions, use them to provoke stories and experiences, even if they seem very tangential to the story.

- Be prepared with multiple articles. Some articles may not be effective in triggering stories for all people. When people become more accustomed to scanning for their stories, even very obtuse articles will produce results. It's a good idea to always have backup articles that are good story instigators.

- Give people time to read the article on their own and record their stories. Then have them try to do the same thing when they are listening to someone. Reading an article and recording stories is easier than listening to someone and sharing stories. The latter is more realistic, but you may want to build up to it by giving people a chance to succeed safely on their own first.

Applications

1. Use this activity in employee orientation programs to break the ice and give people an opportunity to share something personal in a safe manner.

2. This is a great interactive activity for town hall meetings when new announcements are being made. Build in time for people in smaller groups to react to the announcement by sharing their organizational experiences that relate to the information being disseminated. Whenever possible, build in time for people to share some of these with the whole assembly. **Caution:** this can be tricky to do and requires a facilitator to lead and limit the time of the large group discussion. There are still benefits to allowing small group discussions. These can be done without taking a lot of time out of the agenda and without risking difficult-to-manage dynamics that could arise from people reporting out their stories to the whole town hall assembly.

3. Incorporate a variation of this activity during strategic brainstorming sessions, for example, if an organization were considering adopting a new technology and analysts had reviewed white papers. Before using standard conceptual brainstorming techniques with the group such as mind mapping, invite people to respond to the white paper by sharing stories. This will ferret out people's assumptions and attitudes that guide them during the decision-making process but rarely surface as stories. It is much easier to work with people's stories as encoders of their opinions and biases then to go through the charade of an objective process driven by irrational thought processes out of view from the rest of the group.

Case Study

The most powerful experience I ever had with this activity occurred shortly after the September 11, 2001, terrorist attack on the World Trade Center in New York and the Pentagon building. I was in the Washington, D.C., area facilitating a leadership retreat for senior executives of a large organization. All the newspapers were filled with articles about the tragedy. People were in a fog. I had a lot of ground to cover during the retreat, but I realized I would get nowhere if the group didn't have a chance to respond and react to the onslaught of stories stirring inside of themselves. I decided to risk opening the Pandora's Box of raw emotions and try this activity.

I picked three different stories from the *Washington Post* and formed three groups. The articles were very different in nature and represented a wide range of perspectives. One person in the group started reading the article, and as soon as someone had a story triggered by what was being read he or she shared it with the group. If the story triggered others from the group, these stories were all shared before reading the article was resumed. Given the format of the activity, readers were encouraged to share their stories. Every group had a "watcher" appointed. The "watcher's" job was to make sure stories were being shared and not just editorial discussions. We set some ground rules to ensure that the "watchers" were empowered to ask anyone not sharing a story to hold off from voicing his or her thoughts.

Within minutes the room was buzzing with stories. A patchwork of personal associations emerged. Tears commingled with rage, and empathy spurred hope. The newspaper articles served as a framework for amassing a collection of stories. There were stories about friends and families who had died and stories of others who had somehow escaped. There were even "counter-stories" expressing anger toward the United States, which provided a backdrop of unexpected views for people to consider. And then there were stories of how people were coping with their feelings. I remember one person describing going to see the revival of "The Music Man" on Broadway in New York City a couple of weeks after the tragedy. She had been unable to sleep and could not seem to find any way to manage her grief. During the show's finale, the cast came out playing trombones and the American flag unfurled behind the actors. She said the theater erupted in an instantaneous surge of electricity. Without any prompting, every person in the theater stood up at the same time and started yelling and cheering at the top of their lungs. She described the tears rolling down her cheeks while for the first time her muted voice of pain was joined in a chorus of optimism. It was a luminous moment of community catharsis she had been aching for. Mesmerized by her retelling of this story, no one even noticed until she was finished that she had stood up and had tears rolling down her checks. The group bonded in ways that surprised all of us.

The retreat was a huge success. The groundwork for raising people's awareness of the power of stories was laid better than I could have ever architected it. People realized that stories are an invaluable tool for improving communication and building relationships, especially for those in leadership roles.

Relic

Relic

Background

I was eating dinner at one of my favorite restaurants in Boston, glowing in the company of my beautiful fiancée Cindy. We were engrossed in an enthusing discussion of our future together and wedding plans. Despite the fact that I am not a detail person by nature, I took great pride in carefully collaborating with Cindy to architect every aspect of our ceremony and reception. I never knew either one of my grandfathers. Although Grandpa Francesco died when my mother was a little girl and she has few memories of him, he has played an important role in my life. I wanted grandpa to be a part of our wedding ceremony. Cindy suggested I find something that belonged to my grandfather and bring it to the ceremony. I thought this was a great idea. After a long search, my Aunt Maria produced the only possession of my grandfather known to be in existence. It was an old rusted pocket knife that he used to carry around with him everywhere. The knife prompted a flood of memories for my mother and aunt. They recalled how during the great depression my grandfather would entertain six children by cutting a piece of fruit with the knife and telling stories. Ah stories. . . .

Facilitation Level
Easy

Objectives
1. Create a safe and fun vehicle for people to share something personal.
2. Use an object to trigger stories.
3. Gain insight into stories that have had a formative impact on us.

Materials
- Each participant brings an object of personal significance

Time
Three minutes per person, plus five to ten minutes for debriefing

Directions

1. Ask people to bring in an object that has personal significance to them. Explain to people that they will need to share a story about the object.

2. Begin the activity the next day by sharing an object of your own and stories associated with it.

3. Have people take turns sharing their objects and stories.

4. Debrief the experience.

Debriefing

- Even for people who claim to have no stories, this activity shows them that they have stories that are interesting to others and that overlap with the stories of others.

- After you go through everyone's stories, give people a chance to comment on their observations and reactions to the process. More stories and insights surface during this part of the discussion.

- *Why do personal objects invoke strong feelings?* The objects by themselves have no power. They are triggers for our memories and experiences. They are gatekeepers to layers of subjective meaning. Our stories give us direct access to these constructs. Through our stories, we have the control to revisit formative events during which we have acquired some of the raw ingredients comprising our emotional makeup. Objects help us to materialize and solidify our stories. They are monuments we erect for ourselves and others to see. They give us something tangible to share with others. When we revisit personal objects of importance through dialogue, it promotes insights. It allows us to connect our experiences to the experience of others.

- *Do you feel a different dynamic in the group after this activity?* People will feel closer. Sharing a personal object and the stories associated with it opens us up to each other. The boundaries we are accustomed to maintaining between ourselves and others are broken down. We become more real and accessible to each other when we are vulnerable. An external object provides us with the means to share something personal. It doesn't feel onerous. Being vulnerable satisfies one of our greatest needs—we want to feel accepted by others and connected to them. Groups will warm up to each other after this activity. We become more interesting in each others' eyes.

Variations

- Ask people to bring in a piece of music that has personal significance.
- Ask people to share a quote or passage of writing that has significance. You may want to lay down some ground rules for this variation. If you feel anyone

in the group would be offended or ostracized by a religious quote of any tradition, request that people refrain from using them.

- Do the activity in groups of four. Have each group select one person's object and stories to share with the group. Someone else in the group must share with the group at large his or her group member's object and stories.

- Use this activity as a working lunch activity. Turn it into a potluck lunch where every person brings in a dish (or at least a recipe for the dish) that has personal significance to them and shares the stories associated with it.

- For a short, fun, yet interesting twist, ask people to select an object from their workplace environment. This can yield a revealing and engaging discussion about the organization's values, ethos, and current state of affairs.

- Have everyone bring in their objects in bags. This adds an element of surprise and prevents people from learning who the owner of an object is. Lay out all of the objects on a table in front of the group. Have people guess who each object belongs to. Tally the votes and then lead a short discussion during which people throw out stories that they think might be associated with the object. Ask the person who belongs to the object to identify him/herself and share his or her story.

- Instruct people to write down the stories associated with their objects. Set up all the objects on a table. Make copies of all the stories and hand them out. Give people ten to fifteen minutes to walk around the table and read the stories—in silence. Then give people ten to fifteen minutes to mingle with each other. Instruct people to speak with a person whose object or story resonated with them. Have them explore this connection. Debrief the group at large at the end.

Tips

- This activity will generate vulnerability without forcing it. People will feel closer to one another. Use this to the group's benefit. Avoid trying to artificially sustain the community feeling people will have after this activity. Instead, the energy of this activity allows you to help a group surface its differences. You do not need to surface differences with a group if the session's objectives or your comfort level does not permit it. This is a fun, feel-good activity that promotes new bonds, a new appreciation for one another, and that illustrates the communication power of stories are a great set of outcomes—you can stop there. However, if you need to work through any challenging issues, this activity preps the group for such work.

- Gentle teasing is an excellent way to soften the threat of vulnerability for people who might feel overwhelmed by the personal nature of this activity. Better yet, try to goad and guide the group to kid one another and laugh with each other.

- When people share a story, try to get them to tell more than one by asking probing questions. This will help them discover new insights and relationships between their stories.

- If the majority of the group is engaged and the energy level is high, the activity is working well. If you sense any detachment or boredom from any members of the group, it is most likely a defense mechanism. It's unlikely you will succeed in reaching a person responding this way. Rest assured the activity will still have an affect, even if you do not get to see its impact.

Applications

1. This is a great team-building activity that can be used in a variety of situations.

2. Incorporate the activity as part of a project kickoff meeting.

3. Use this activity at the beginning of a standing meeting. This even works for virtual meetings (e.g., conference calls or web-based formats). For this application, especially if it's virtual, I like to ask people to share a quote with the group and a story around it. I then give people an opportunity to respond to the quote and explore any applicability of the quote to the group, its work objectives, and the meeting's agenda. Take comments only and don't be drawn into a long, protracted discussion. Reserve the full discussion for its appropriate place in the meeting.

Case Study

At the end of the second day of a five-day leadership retreat I was leading, I gave people the assignment. Jack, a vice president of operations and a no-nonsense kind of guy, gave me a funny look, but didn't say anything. A major thrust of our discussions during the retreat centered on the importance of relationships. One of Jack's goals at the beginning of the retreat was to learn new ways he could foster more open relationships with his staff. This was confirmed by the 360-degree feedback surveys I had collected and the interviews with his staff that I had done. After sharing an object and story of my own, I asked for a volunteer. I was surprised when Jack was excited to go first and walked to the front opening of the large oval, U-shaped configuration of chairs. Jack produced a small plaster foot impression from his pocket and began to tell us his story:

> Seven years ago, little Rudy was born. My sister's husband died in a tragic accident before the baby was even born. She pleaded with me to be a father to her unborn child. I had no idea what that meant. I was a bachelor at

the time and had no intention of having children. I took her earnest request to heart, but I turned out to be a pretty mediocre surrogate father. Poopy diapers were not my thing. While I was as loving and supportive of my sister as best as I could be, I really didn't have a clue how to be there for Rudy and her. I kept telling myself and her that when Rudy was bigger it would easier for me to play a more active role in his life. I talked about the football and baseball games we would go to. Three weeks after Rudy's second birthday, he died. Rudy's heart never developed properly, despite doctors' best efforts. Rudy and his mom gave me this plaster foot as a Father's Day present. I keep it in my bedroom as a reminder. I'm a father now and not a day goes by I don't think of Rudy and vow to be the best father I can possibly be to my son.

When I went home last night I was afraid to share this plaster foot and its poignant story with you, but I realized something. I am guilty of doing the same thing at work sometimes that I did with Rudy and his mom. I don't want to repeat the same mistake in a different area of my life.

There was a stunned silence in the room and Jack, who had been holding his emotions in check, walked back to his seat and put his head in his hands.

Stories in Words

Stories in Words

Background

I was attending a storytelling conference at the Smithsonian and I heard a wonderful presentation by Madelyn Blair of Pelerei, Inc. She spoke about the power and poetry of words. She demonstrated how words are containers for stories. Madelyn has done some fascinating work with ambassadors to the United Nations (UN). She shared the details of one intervention in which she asked ambassadors to identify a word from the preamble to the UN Charter that was important to them and to tell a story triggered by that word. She played some examples for us, and the stories were mesmerizing. (More on her project and its future can be found at www.Pelerei.com.) I have used a similar process in my work with organizations and their mission statements, but as I listened to Madelyn I was struck by the applicability of this process for individuals. So I designed an activity.

Facilitation Level
Moderate

Objectives
1. Use words to trigger stories and connections.
2. Increase awareness of how words can be used to index stories.
3. Encourage associations and linkages between people and ideas.

Materials
- Copies of the organization's mission statement

Time
Thirty to forty-five minutes

Directions
1. Hand out a copy of the organization's mission statement.
2. Instruct people to read it and circle words or short phrases that are important to them.
3. Give people ten minutes to jot down stories (experiences they have had that are triggered by the words they circled).

4. Break into groups of four and ask people to share their stories.

5. Debrief the activity.

Debriefing

- When using an organizational mission statement, people may have difficulty thinking of stories. They may even resent the mission statement. It's not uncommon for people to feel disconnected from them. Mission statements express lofty ideals, so the larger the perceived gap between the statement and reality the more resistant people will be to the activity. This is not a bad thing, and it can be leveraged to generate rich dialogue. You can begin to address people's feelings of disenfranchisement from the organization through this activity. It's rare to have a group without any individuals who have positive stories that exemplify words from the mission statement. Lean on these stories. Don't dismiss or minimize people's frustrations. Dwell on the positive stories. This will help people re-engage with the organization's strengths and discover how they might rekindle and refashion these foundational strengths through their own roles in the organization and daily contributions. This is a good time for people to share organizational lore. These are stories that are part of the organization's history that people have heard. Examine how relevant those stories are to the organization today.

- People will latch onto different words and for different reasons. Encourage and promote this diversity of reactions. Remind people that we index information in different ways.

- *How are stories contained in words?* Words are how we index and retrieve our experiences, defining what a story is relative to the context and the audience with which it is being shared. A word can encapsulate a whole universe of stories. Words open the door to our memories and recollections. Words are the links to stimulating these associations. If we are to become more mindful of our stories, we need to become more mindful of how we index and retrieve them. Experiencing the power of words for triggering stories gives us a ready-made tool to use that is the backbone of our communication.

- *Why do we care about triggering stories with words?* Meaning is found and constructed from our collection of stories. We are continually assimilating and linking patterns of stories to inform our thoughts and guide our actions. Words are all around us. If we become accustomed to using words to become more reflective in the moment of our stories, we will increase the potency of our communications. We will be more in tune with ourselves and better able to reach out to others. When stories are at the forefront of our consciousness, whether we are "telling" them all the time or not, we are better capable of connecting to others.

Stories in Words

Variations

- Have people write personal mission statements. For example, mine is, *"I have a passion for inciting insight in others."*

- Have people write personal "organizational" mission statements. These describe their purpose and role in the organization and how they make a difference. For example,

  "My purpose is to express my commitment to quality, perseverance, and business savvy by ensuring my customers always get the best, by keeping on track with my goals, and by staying on top of the latest industry trends to create an ever-increasing customer base, a new customer incentive program, a monthly business development meeting with my associates, and at least $1.5 million in gross revenue by this date one year from today." (Source: www.nightingale.com/tMission_ExampleStatement.asp)

- Ask people to write a new mission statement for their organization. Have people swap mission statements with one another.

- Hand out a sheet of mission statements from well-known companies and ask people to select one. Have them circle key words or phrases. Have them jot down their stories and then share with partners.

- Do the activity with Story Collages™. This works best if people have used them before.

Tips

- Hand out a hard copy of the mission statement. Read the mission statement out loud once. I usually let someone in the group do this and then let people work by themselves. If people start making comments about the mission statement, defer them until the final debriefing. You do not want anyone's comments to impact people's responses to the mission statement.

- For people struggling, try reframing the activity for them. Try questions like, *What words are important to you in the mission statement? Are there any words that you'd like to see the organization embrace more? Can you think of any recent experiences that are examples of the organization failing to live up to its mission?*

- Counter-stories can be used in juxtaposition to positive ones to stimulate conversation. One negative story can even block people from recounting positives ones, even when they have them. If there is a flood of negative stories, use these to imagine how the mission statement can be better actualized.

- Personal mission statements can be hard for people to write, but stories can help them hone in on what is important to them. Have people use Story

142

Collage™ or another brainstorming technique such as mind mapping to capture either a collection of stories or list of things that are important to them. Help people write one-to-four-sentence mission statements. They should be something that they can commit to memory and share easily. I also tell people to imagine what they want people to say about them after they pass away.

- "Personal" organizational mission statements are a great way to invigorate people to see how they are essential assets to the organization. When I am debriefing this version of the activity, I project the organizational mission statement and hand out a copy of it. I tell everyone to copy their "personal" organizational mission statements next to it. Then I'll go around the room and ask people to share the relationships they see between the two. This will lead to more stories.

Applications

1. Incorporate this activity into employee orientation and board of directors' initiation programs. I've videotaped senior leaders of the organization sharing their key words and stories. It also makes a great follow-up discussion to ask people to describe the new role they are assuming and how they see themselves supporting the organization's mission through it. Make these stories available on an intranet site. Be sure to give people the ability to add their comments or stories.

2. Do this activity every year as the open part of an organization's strategic planning meeting.

3. Use this activity during marketing focus groups conducted with external customers.

Case Study

I sat down one day with Carol Biddle, the executive director of the Kinship Center, and asked her to do this activity with me. Here's what she had to say:

Kinship Center Mission Statement

Kinship Center is dedicated to supporting the creation and preservation of foster, adoptive, and related families for children who need them.

Keyword for Carol—Preservation

Carol's Story

In the late 1980s, Kinship Center had less than five years of history as a licensed agency when this crisis/opportunity presented itself.

One of those "Friday afternoons in child welfare" calls came regarding a two-year-old medically fragile child who had spent months, off and on, in a major teaching hospital. She had been alternately in foster care, with her very young single mother, and back into the hospital because of her multiple medical disabilities. When Kari was released from a regional teaching hospital, she was taken into protective custody again because her young mother could not care for her, although she tried. Kari's disabilities included an uncorrected cleft palate (severe), various congenital anomalies, and a requirement that she be fed through a tube inserted into her throat (she could not swallow).

Miraculously, there was a willing foster family, the Bakers, who had cared for children with cleft palates and those requiring feeding tubes. The county social worker carried the child into the foster home, and all present were appalled to see a two-year-old who weighed less than twelve pounds, wrapped in a receiving blanket and wearing only an infant T-shirt and diaper.

The fragile child was taken to the local hospital to be evaluated by a pediatrician. The physician and hospital staff spent several hours evaluating the child and instructing the foster mother on inserting the feeding tube successfully. Kari was discharged to the foster mother's care with appointments for regular follow-up.

Within weeks, Kari began to gain weight and settle into this unusual and dedicated family. She was scheduled for an appointment at Stanford Medical Center for evaluation and to determine the feasibility of future surgery to make her feeding easier. The foster family adored this little girl. Kari's foster mother, Diane, transported her in a front-loaded infant carrier for months. Kari was initially so small and still that the carrier, under a coat, made Diane look pregnant. This tiny child gradually gained weight and became responsive. She would even occasionally smile and look into Diane's eyes. Kinship Center staff was gratified and delighted with her care and progress.

Kari eventually had surgery, allowing her to be fed through a "G" tube in her stomach. However, a state licensing worker visited the home and declared that this child needed institutional care and would need to be moved immediately. With some feelings of distress, the dilemma was presented to the board of directors, with the Kinship Center staff recommendation that this child not be moved again because she was doing so well and because of her need to continue her healthy attachment to this family. The agency's pediatric consultant supported the staff recommendation. The board members recommended and supported a formal appeals process to the licensing agency, giving Kinship Center a chance to keep this child safely placed in a family.

The appeals process continued for more than one year, with volumes of paperwork and the state sending consulting physicians to see the child. The net result was that the child was allowed to stay in the foster home, but the ruling was "not considered to be a precedent." The foster family adopted Kari. Ultimately, Kari died at age twelve of complications of her fragile physical and developmental disabilities. The actual results were much larger than extending her life and providing her with a family, although that would have been a sufficient outcome. Kari became an inspiration to her family, her church and school community, and to the staff and board at Kinship Center. She had the highest quality of life that could be given to her, was a happy child, and shared lessons about normalizing care for developmentally disabled children to all whose lives she touched.

Beyond the happy family outcome, for Kinship Center, the lasting lesson was discovering the courage to dissent and to challenge, at the risk of losing state licensing. When faced with adversity, the measurement of the agency's mission impelled courage, determination, and an organizational life lesson about advocacy. Kari provided an early and significant learning opportunity about claiming the stated values that were integral to the mission of the organization.

Story Collage™

Story Collage™

Background

After a day of running a grueling communications workshop, I went back to my hotel room feeling sad. The participants were struggling and I knew I had to try something different. I was desperately trying to get people to share their experiences with one another, but no one was speaking up. People were complaining, "We have no stories to tell." Even worse, the few stories that had been shared were random and unconnected to each other and not very cogent to the themes of the workshop.

Exhausted, I slumped into my chair. "People are walking treasure chests of stories," I thought to myself. "How can I help them discover their stories and see the relationships between them?" I sat down with my ever-handy composition book and began to doodle. That afternoon I created a tool called Story Collage™ for facilitating story brainstorming and reflection.

Facilitation Level
Easy

Objectives
1. Help people discover and organize their stories.
2. Reflect on stories and look for relationships between them.
3. Promote dialogue, sharing, and learning from each other's stories.

Materials
- Blank Story Collage™ handout
- Sample Story Collage™ handout

Note: Copies of the blank form as well as filled-out samples can be found on the accompanying CD-ROM.

Time
Fifteen to ninety minutes (depending on how it's being used)

Directions

1. Distribute a copy of the blank Story Collage™ handout as well as a sample filled-in form to each participant.

2. Provide a topic for the Story Collage™. This will serve as the Story Circle.

3. Instruct people to jot down short descriptions of their stories and other words they associate with the story that jar their recall of it. These short descriptions are referred to as Story Hubs.

4. Guide people to look at all their Story Hubs and build an index of keywords that characterize the stories.

5. Have people share their Story Collage™ with each other. Ask them to explore how their Story Collage™ relate to one another.

6. Debrief the activity.

Note: The figure below shows the placement of the various elements of the Story Collage™.

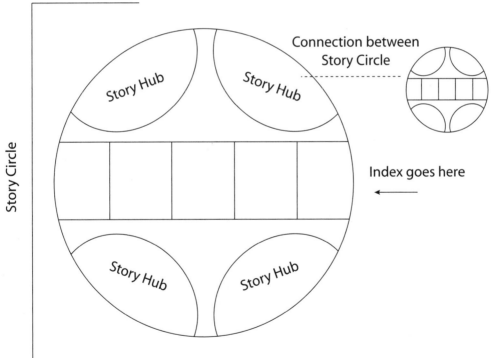

Story Collage™

Debriefing

- When debriefing the activity, start with some process-related questions, for example, "How did that go? What did you notice during the process? Were there any surprises? Did you find any part of this activity difficult?" These are just sample questions. There's no need to ask all of them, but you do want to give people an opportunity to react to the process (positive, negative, and neutral) before diving into people's stories and the connections and relationships between them that they discovered. If ideas of how to improve the process emerge during the debriefing process, be sure to record them and if possible make a commitment to incorporate them the next time you run the activity.

- Always try to get people to share other people's stories. For example, if someone is describing an insight she had or a connection he discovered between his or her story and someone else's, ask the person to recount the other person's story. Be sure to check back with the original storyteller to get his or her perspective.

- *Did people remember new stories?* Most of us are not in the habit of recalling our experiences as stories to share with others. Story Collage™ provides people with a guided process to discover their stories and see the connections between their stories and the stories of others. Encourage people to think about their stories and to be more mindful of sharing them with others.

- *How do the index of key words in the Story Collage™ relate to the stories? Do people have similar indices?* Everyone unconsciously builds a unique index associated with their experiences. We do not think about how we are indexing experiences. We make the naïve assumption that others have indexed their experiences in a similar way. This creates breakdowns in communication and understanding. Stories help us bridge the gaps created by didactic modes of conversation. However, we need to be sensitive to the different ways we classify our experiences. I may not be able to recall an experience if you ask me to recall it by utilizing your schema. The richer your index, the easier it will be for you to find a relevant experience to share or determine the best language for eliciting stories from others.

- *How does the index in the Story Collage™ help people reflect on their experiences?* We are not computer databases; therefore, indexing single experiences is neither necessary nor desirable. Story Collage™ captures a collection of stories. The indexing process helps people to quickly begin thinking about the interrelationships between their stories. By indexing the collection of stories, it becomes easier to recall one or more of the stories in the future and see connections with stories from other areas of our lives and experience. The index also makes it easier for us to see parallel themes in other people's stories.

Variations

- Try this activity with small groups instead of individuals. This is a great way to get a heterogeneous group of people to learn from each others' experiences and perspectives. For example, I have divided participants into groups of managers and employees.

- Facilitate a group discussion to decide the topic for a Story Collage™.

- Share a personal Story Collage™ with the group as an example. Alternatively, feel free to use the samples provided on the CD-ROM accompanying this book.

- Have a group discuss a manager's or leader's Story Collage™. Use the manager's collage to elicit stories from participants.

- Assign Story Collage™ as pre-work or homework.

- Create the Story Collage™ on butcher block paper and have participants take a tour around the room to share short dialogues about each others' stories.

- Shorten or lengthen the time of the activity.

- Ask people to do a Story Collage™ before a major group discussion in which you hope to get people to share their personal experiences. This is a great way to help people collect their thoughts.

- Use Story Collages™ instead of a concept map (e.g., Mind Map) to help people prepare a written or oral presentation.

Tips

- People index their stories in different ways. Be sure the topic for the Story Collage™ is broad enough that it triggers stories for them. A short phrase versus a single word will yield a richer collection of experiences. For example, if I want people to recount their experiences after a multi-day sales meeting, I might use a phrase like, *"Significant conversations that stick out in my mind from the last few days,"* for my Story Circle. This phrase will be more effective than, *"My sales meeting experience."*

- Invite people to suggest topics. You can use a variety of facilitation techniques to do this. For example, you might have everyone write two or three short phrases. List all of the topics and look for ones that naturally group. Then take proposals from the group as to which one or ones they want to work on. If you are having difficulty getting the group to agree on one topic, then take a vote and select the top two or three.

- Try playing some quiet, relaxing instrumental music in the background while people work.

- Circulate in the room while people are working on their collages. Help people who seem to be struggling to find stories. Before breaking people into pairs or groups, make sure people have some stories to share. You don't want to group two people together who have very few stories. At least one member of a pair or group should have a healthy number of stories to share.

- If you are using this activity to help a group better understand its members and dynamics impacting it, visually capture the relationships between the Story Collage™. This can be done by drawing lines or by using string and push pins to connect story hubs between collages, drawing symbols, using colored sticky pads, creating summary lists, or any other visually summarizing strategy. This becomes a critical map and summary for the group that it can refer back to later.

Applications
1. Incorporate Story Collage™ into business processes (e.g., performance reviews, after action reviews, employee orientations, product development, and marketing focus groups).
2. Instill standard story sharing, dialogue, and reflection with groups.
3. Harvest key stories to promote knowledge sharing.

Case Study

It was the end of the day and I picked up the phone to answer the sort of call I dread. One of my regular clients was frantic, "Hey, Terrence, I've got some serious issues going on here. My project team is falling apart. I've spent all day in meetings with folks trying to sort out a tangled mess of problems, but with no success. Everyone is up in arms. Lots of finger pointing going on, and I haven't been able to get to the bottom of it. I've called an emergency meeting for tomorrow morning. I know you haven't been involved with the project, but will you please come in and facilitate? There will be thirty people from three different functional areas. Can I count on you?"

Walking into a lion's den is never my first choice, but this client was desperate. I mumbled into the receiver, "Okay, you can count on me."

The next morning I walked into a board room teeming with emotions. With very little in the way of introduction, I pulled out a stack of blank Story Collage™ forms and broke the group into five teams of six, with two representatives from each functional area on each team. I instructed people to work in pairs from the same functional area and record their frustrating experiences to date on the project. I gave them about fifteen minutes to work. Then I asked them to find some key words to characterize their collection of stories. Next I had the teams of six assemble to share their collages with each other and develop a summary. When I regrouped all of the teams, there was an amazing new energy in the room. People were bubbling over with ideas and insights. Misperceptions, untold stories, dependencies between people's responsibilities, and unrealized hurt feelings all came rushing out in a stream of stories. The collages had helped people surface their emotions and assumptions in a safe and thorough fashion while simultaneously providing them opportunities to see the situation from very different perspectives. By the end of all the sharing, with no prompting on my part, people were ready to dive into a litany of recommendations.

Story Scrap Booking

Story Scrap Booking

Background

Thank heavens for big sisters, especially mine. I was over at Franca's house sipping hot chocolate and catching up on life. While we spoke, she was immersed in assembling another one of her family scrap book masterpieces. I'm one of those unfortunate types who love trips down family memory lane but lack the discipline and patience to keep scrap books. We started talking about Franca's work. She is an international marketing and publication relations consultant. As we discussed the internal communication challenges one of her clients was facing, I had a flash of brilliance. What if we helped the client put together a story scrap book and then used it to facilitate conversations around the organization? That's exactly what we did and with fantastic results. Since then it has become one of the standard tools and interventions I use. I adapted the process so that it works as an activity that can be used with individuals as well as groups.

Facilitation Level
Moderate

Objectives
1. Create a conversation piece to encourage open communication.
2. Capture key stories to examine the connections between them and transfer knowledge.
3. Use stories to promote self-awareness and active sense making.

Materials
- A timeline for each participant

Time
Sixty to ninety minutes

Directions
1. Hand out timelines to help people trigger and capture their stories for the past year. I give people a four-page handout with the names of three months on each page.

2. Ask people to think back on the year and record descriptions of their stories around key events.

3. Break them into groups of six to eight people and have them share scrap books.

4. Debrief the activity by having each group report out.

Debriefing

- *How do story scrap books encourage meaningful conversations?* Story scrap books promote reflection. As we create them, we remember our experiences and uncover new insights in the process. People respond to scrap books with stories. Our scrap book is a ritualistic object that achieves its highest purpose when we use it to facilitate dialogue with others. Scrap books promote community because they are shared records of identity. Think about how a family photo album functions. Our stories trigger other people's stories. Through a dynamic exchange of stories, our conversations become insightful gold mines full of authentic pieces of ourselves. We see ourselves for how we are and we generate meaning from how we reflect on our stories and how others respond to them.

- *How do story scrap books help transfer knowledge?* The most valuable information in an organization is unstructured data. This is data that lives in the minds and experiences of people. It is not easily captured or stored in central repositories. Furthermore, in most organizations there are few if any incentives to share knowledge. As a result, knowledge sits untapped. People do not speak with one another in ways that enable knowledge to flow. Stories activate informal peer-to-peer networks. The scrap books are wonderful tools for recording and transferring knowledge. Every story chronicled in a scrap book has relation to other stories. The collection of stories forms a cluster of knowledge that can be tapped. Patterns of organizational best practices, experiences, and encoded organizational cultural values reside in these clusters of knowledge. Through dialogue, these can be clarified, brought to a focus, and cultivated to inform future successful behavior.

Variations

- Modify the time period. For a shorter activity, try decreasing the time period.

- Give this as a pre-event homework assignment.

- Give this as an assignment at the beginning of a multi-day learning event. Provide people a little time every day to work on their scrap books. Share the scrap books on the last day.

- Instead of breaking into small groups, have everyone share a few stories from their scrap books with the group at large. Allow people to respond to each other stories by sharing a story from their own scrap books triggered by someone else's. Frequently people have the same story to tell from a different perspective.
- Create actual books with pictures and other pieces of memorabilia.
- Share scrap books as part of a working lunch at a learning event.
- Share scrap books as part of a brown-bag lunch series.
- Create electronic versions of the scrap books with audio clips, pictures, video, and text. Post these on an intranet site.
- Assemble a scrap book of organizational leaders' stories in advance of an event. Ask these people to come and share their stories with the group. Use their stories to trigger stories from the group and promote dialogue between leaders and employees.

Tips

- Create your own scrap book ahead of time to share with a group when you give them the assignment.
- Timelines are a good tool for helping people to trigger stories, but you may need to try some other techniques as well, for example, try coaching people to think about the major projects they worked on over the year.
- When doing this as an individual activity, I encourage people to include work and personal stories in the same scrap book. There are often unexpected connections between the two types of stories, and people enjoy sharing them.
- This activity does a good job of running itself. While it can be very personal for people, it is also fun. People's greatest benefit comes from sharing their scrap books in groups. For people concerned about their privacy, ensure them they will not have to share anything they do not want to. The scrap book will be valuable as a reflective record for them, even if they do not want to share everything in it. Except for the most extreme cases, encourage people you detect are concerned about being private to share some of their work-related stories.
- Revisiting this activity the next day yields new insights and discussions.
- This is a retrospective activity. It helps people look back and reflect on their experiences. When this is used with a team or work group, it provides them with an excellent snapshot of where they have been. Groups can use the stories to project how they want to navigate the future.

Applications

1. Incorporate this activity as a part of a team retreat.

2. Use this as a group process during after-action reviews for large-scale projects or end-of-year discussions. It's an excellent tool for promoting knowledge transfer.

3. Weave a variation of this activity into strategic planning processes.

Case Study

The CEO pulled me into his office and closed the door. He had just spent a mint on printing ten thousand extra copies of the company's annual report. He motioned me to take a seat and dropped one of the annual reports on my lap with a beaming grin of satisfaction. "You're going to like this," he said. "I want every employee to be proud of our accomplishments, so I am distributing a copy of this report to every employee. I'm having all my VPs go around the company to hand these out during special town hall meetings. This is just the sort of thing that will get people fired up to exceed next year's goals."

I had already seen the annual report and, despite its spectacular design, stunning photographs, and stellar numbers, it was as drab as drab can be. I was nonplussed. It was the right idea but the wrong tool. I acknowledged the merits of his strategy and then I asked him if he was open to trying an experiment. He asked me what I had in mind. I told him to identify a division or area of the company that was going to be critical to the achievement of next year's goals. There were some unused days on my monthly retainer that were going to expire, so I asked him for a couple of days to do some digging. I held a couple of meetings with groups of people from the division and ran them through a version of this activity. I started each meeting by handing out the annual reports and asking people to thumb through them, looking at the key objectives that had been achieved during the year. Then I asked them to develop a story scrap book for the year that captured their personal experiences of how they had played a role in the achievement of these key objectives. Next I scheduled a town hall meeting for the entire division and invited the CEO to attend. I asked two people with very compelling story scrap books to share them with the group. Then I gave everyone ten minutes to speak to the person next to them and share their experiences. I reconvened the group and opened the floor for ten minutes so that people could share some of the stories they had heard. Finally, I had the CEO briefly share the organization's new goals and ask people to imagine how their stories next year would be different. We were thrilled by people's energy. We succeeded in engaging people's imaginations. I coached some of the CEO's directors and VPs, and we rolled out a similar process across the entire organization.

Study Tour

Study Tour

Background

It was the hottest day of summer on the East Coast and the air conditioner broke. It was bad enough twenty people were crammed in a hotel conference room designed for twelve people or fewer. The heat was getting to me and I needed to come up with a solution quickly. Patience and good humor would not be enough in this situation. We had a lot of ground to cover and I couldn't afford to lose any time with the group, but there was also no way I could ask them to work in our room that was rapidly turning into an oven. From our room's window I eyed a large shopping mall across the street and I had an idea.

Facilitation Level
Difficult

Objectives
1. Become aware of how perceptions are formed.
2. Generate alternative interpretations of observations.
3. Engage in dialogue to verify and expand initial perceptions.

Materials
- None

Time
Sixty minutes

Directions
1. Put people into groups of two or three.
2. Take teams to a busy public place.
3. Give them half an hour and instruct them to observe and discuss at least two to three interactions.
4. Debrief the experience.

Debriefing

- After observing an interaction on their study tour, groups should discuss their perceptions. Instruct the groups to probe each other to explain how they formed their perceptions.

- Appoint a spokesperson from each group to share the story of their study tour. Ask other members of the group to refrain from commenting until the spokesperson is done. Then solicit feedback from the rest of the group. Even within a short period of time and with a small group, perceptions will shift. Be aware that people will be surprised—even upset with the spokesperson if he or she fails to adequately capture the group's experience. Watch for subtle body language and speech cues to detect people's reactions. This is a key learning component of the activity, so bring it to people's attention without making anyone feel self-conscious or bad.

- After a group shares an observation, poll the group at large for alternative interpretations. When an alternative one is offered, ask the person to explain how he or she arrived at it.

- *Why does the same observation lead to different interpretations?* We spend our lives making sense of what we observe around us. These are, in essence, stories. They are theories we generate to explain what we see, and they influence our behaviors, although usually on an unconscious level. Perceptual filters play a major role influencing how we interpret things around us. Because we have different experiences, our perceptual filters vary greatly. Therefore we are apt to interpret things differently. When we become aware of our perceptual filters and how they bias our interpretations, we can censor them to prevent them from interfering with our experience of the world. Our stories become allies instead of potential stumbling blocks that can get in the way of our communicating and connecting with others.

- *What role does dialogue play in expanding our perceptions?* Dialogue opens the door for us to verify and expand our interpretations. While we rely on our interpretations to guide our actions and words with others, they are never complete and can be wrong. Sharing our perceptions with others enables us to learn from them. Dialogue invites possibilities and encourages us to be humble. We become sensitive to a multiplicity of perspectives. Dealt with as stories, these multiple perspectives will not dilute or confuse our dominant points of view. It is easier to work with stories to understand someone else's viewpoint that competes with our own. Stories help to momentarily suspend our judgments. We end up listening to people's stories instead of comparing or defending our cherished opinions. Stories act as enhancers so that our perspective is deepened by a widening array of viewpoints. Having other people to dialogue with about our perceptions is ideal, but we can accomplish the same effect through internal dialogue.

Variations
- Do this activity over a lunch break.
- Conduct the study tour at the organization. Request permission for your participants to attend part of a meeting in a different part of the organization.
- For multi-day events, give this as a homework assignment.
- Try a reversal of the activity. Have two to three outside naïve observers visit your group during your session. Ask them to share their perceptions of the group and its interactions. Create a list of questions for the observers to help focus their attention.

Tips
- Groups will be confused about what they are supposed to watch on their study tour. Anything that catches their attention will work. To simplify this activity when you are running it in public places, instruct the groups to appoint a "spotter." This role can rotate among members of the group. The spotter selects a scene to observe and directs others' attention to it.
- Caution groups not to be intrusive or obvious when they are watching an interaction. The subjects should not know they are being watched.
- Expect some silliness. You never know what people are going to bring back. It can get zany, but be sensitive to maintain boundaries of appropriateness.

Applications
1. Use as a lunch-time activity for any type of workshop.
2. Include this activity in any customer service/call center/help desk learning event.
3. Give this activity as a homework assignment in advance of product development or marketing brainstorming meetings. These study tours should involve products and customers to be discussed during this meeting. Begin the meeting by listening to people's observations.

Case Study

I was leading a product development retreat for a high-tech company. The team of software engineers was energetic, bright, and dedicated to their work. However, it was clear to me that there was a lot of groupthink when it came to the design of the user interface for the application. This did not surprise me. The engineers had had a bad experience with a usability consultancy that had been hired to work with them. As a result, the engineers had become entrenched in their ideas about what was best for the next release of the software. While there was good communication between members of the team, anyone outside the inner sanctum of software engineering was treated with professional respect but distrust.

I had no intention of doing this activity, but I wasn't making much headway with the group. After a day of discussions and brainstorming, the group's leading strategy was to write more test scripts to evaluate the user interface. There was nothing wrong with that strategy; however, it was only part of the solution. I wanted to push their thinking, so I called a friend of mine who worked at a nearby company that I knew used the software. I asked him if I could bring a group of twelve software engineers by the next day. I bribed him with lunch at one of his favorite restaurants, and we were all set.

About half an hour before lunch, the whole gang of us descended upon the company where my friend worked. He was a director of the company's customer care center. He managed a team of sixty-two sales reps who all used my client's software. I broke the engineers into four groups of three and instructed them to roam the floor watching how the reps used the software while interacting with customers on the phone. I encouraged people to take notes, but told them they were not allowed to speak with each other about what they were observing while they were at the company. Believe it or not, for many of these engineers this was the first time they had ever seen the software in a live production environment. After half an hour I corralled the groups of engineers, who were reluctant to leave, and my friend and we headed out to lunch. I instructed the teams to compare their notes with each other's. Lunch was dominated by boisterous discussions. I couldn't wait to get people back to our conference room to hear their perceptions. With the permission of the engineers, I invited my friend to join us for the activity debriefing.

The teams had very similar experiences. They observed sales reps struggling to use some feature of the software while interacting with a customer. At least one person in each team concluded the sales rep was not well trained on the software or inexperienced, while someone else perceived either an awkwardness or flaw in the software's design. With each example, we queried my friend to learn more about how the sales rep had to use the software to address that customer's need. Out of the fifteen examples, eleven pointed to significant opportunities to improve the software. The engineers were amazed at all of the assumptions they had been making and how their failure to consider the software from a variety of perspectives had impacted its design. Through observations and dialogue, the group had moved to a whole new frame of reference. The next version of the software was very well received, and since it made my friend's job easier, it was my turn to get a free lunch out of the deal.

Take Three

Take Three

Background

I love the sounds of things. Perhaps it's my musical background. I can spend hours immersing myself in the intricate interplay of pitches and tones interacting with one another. Sometimes silence is a symphony replete with vibrations crying out to be heard, if we can just attend to them. I am fascinated by how we can move our attention from the disjointed competitive noises that saturate our environment to a place where meanings emerge. I was attending a workshop on stories and complexity in New Mexico not too long ago when I encountered this activity for the first time. One of my colleagues from the STORI Institute, Theodore Tadtipklis, recorded the proceedings of our sessions. On the last day, he selected a three-minute sound byte from the recordings he had taken and asked everyone to listen to it. We repeated this process of listening and discussing what we heard three times, and each time we discovered something new. I have adopted this unique listening process in my workshops and I have been humbled by the depth of connections and insights this activity generates.

Facilitation Level
Easy

Objectives
1. Create a space of listening that slows people down.
2. Penetrate below the surface to hear new shades of meaning.
3. Participate in a dialogue invigorated by deep listening.

Materials
- Recording device
- Playback device
- Also see the sample file on the CD-ROM

Time
Thirty to forty-five minutes

Directions

1. Let people know you'd like to record some of the group's discussion. Explain that it will be used later for a listening exercise and that the recording will not be shared outside of the room.

2. Record about thirty to forty-five minutes of the group's discussion.

3. Select two to three minutes of the recording to replay.

4. Ask people to listen to the recording you have selected. Tell them that you will replay it three to five times. After each playing you will invite people to share their observations.

5. Debrief the group.

Debriefing

- Steer the group away from analyzing each other's observations. It can be easy to get pulled off on tangents. People will want to question the speaker or speakers in the recording. Some of this is okay, but it mustn't dominate the discussion. The discussion is meant to elicit people's observations. You are after observations and not analysis. By the third hearing, if some people have not shared any observations or if the discussions have been dominated by a few people, ask those who haven't spoken to share their observations.

- If the people on the recording are present, ask them to comment on what they remember saying, what they meant by what they said, what they heard themselves saying when they heard it replayed, and their reactions to other people's observations.

- *What changes when we listen to something over and over again?* Once we get past our resistance to listening to the same thing over and over again, we discover a vibrant world of interpretation and meaning. Tones, inflections, pauses, and content stand out. Our awareness is focused and then heightened. Something marvelous happens when we create a community space of listening. People are joined together as a collective ear. Signals are amplified, and whatever lay beneath the surface rushes forward to be discovered and acknowledged by the group. Our preconceived notions are thrust aside. We become witnesses rather than participants. Paradoxically, we are more involved as witnesses than we are as active participants. It's only natural that, as participants in a conversation, we are invested in making ourselves heard and being clear in what we are communicating. Attending to all the subtle nuances of our exchanges requires more bandwidth than any of us have, even if we are earnest and practiced in our efforts to be mindful and good active listeners. During a conversation we are apt to hear what we expect to hear and notice what we want to notice. Our purpose changes when we commit ourselves simply to listening.

We empty ourselves of distractions that trap our attention. We can be present with what is being said. The original conversation we are listening to has moved outside of time. We are revisiting a moment from the past that is unpacked by the group's collection of perceptions. Each person becomes a very sensitive channel capable of picking up things that others cannot. The moment is reborn, and through dialogue new stories find voices.

- *How can this type of listening be practiced in our work and lives?* It can't. This is not to say we shouldn't strive to listen to others this deeply or intently; it's just not realistic nor possible to do this all of the time. The multiplicity of layers of meanings brought forward by the "meta process" of listening, discussing, re-listening, and discussing in a group slows down the original event and is what cannot be replicated outside of this activity. The activity is intended to be an experiential mind opener and a humbling experience. When we temper our communications with a dose of doubt braced by our convictions, we can connect more effectively with others. Our limitations as listeners are necessary boundaries. We'd have a heck of a time interacting with the world if we were in a state of perpetual deep listening with this amount of processing going on all the time. It's too much for one individual to do, but it's not too much for a group to do. Everyone plays a role. Groups with breakthrough communication skills serve as guardians of deep listening for one another. Where there is openness and honesty, people become willing to trust the collective intelligence and listening sensitivities of the group, rather than trying to shoulder it all themselves. The degree of openness present in a group softens people's defensiveness and they are less inclined to challenge each other. It's liberating to accept the fact that we cannot decipher everything we hear when we abandon the myth of thinking we can or should. The benefit of experiencing this type of listening is to encourage people to try harder to hear each other more deeply, to use dialogue with others to discover more nuances of meaning, and to become cognizant of the pregnant possibilities contained in the moment.

Variations
- If you are unable to record or for any reason it is inappropriate to do so in your setting, use the audio file provided on the CD-ROM titled Take Three—Audio.
- For a shorter version of this activity and for a different effect, play a piece of music multiple times and ask people what new things they hear each time.
- Ask the group to select what they want recorded.
- Time permitting and with the group's cooperation, play the segment five times.
- Instead of discussing the segment after each hearing, give people about three minutes of silence to write down their observations.

- Share observations in pairs or small groups after each hearing. End the exercise with a large group discussion.
- Record someone sharing their stories from the Magic Three activity.
- Randomly select the segment you replay to the group.

Tips
- I suggest people close their eyes while listening to the recording. It's not necessary, but many people find it helps them listen better. It's very personal, but it's a good suggestion to offer people.
- Allow some silence after playing the recording. People will need a chance to move their attention back to the room.
- There will be some resistance associated with listening to the same thing over and over again, especially if you ask people to listen to it more than three times. Despite people's reluctance, they will be surprised at the end of the process how many new things they hear each time they listen.
- No need to make any major points during the debriefing. Just work with people's observations. Many of the learnings will occur later. This activity benefits from some time and distance during which people will further reflect on and synthesize their listening experience.
- There are no hard-and-fast rules about how to select a segment to replay to a group. If you are facilitating a multi-day event or if you will have the group together on another occasion, listen to as much of what you have recorded as you possibly can. Take notice of what strikes you and be honest as to why it strikes you. Be careful of selecting a segment that serves your own or anyone else's personal agenda. As a general rule, difficult moments are good candidates.

Applications
1. On a regular basis record part of a meeting. Randomly select a two-minute sound byte to play at the next meeting. Start the meeting with this activity as a way of getting people focused and tuned in to each other. It's critical to set strong ground rules of minimal analysis and that whatever is replayed mustn't be used as fodder during the current meeting. In other words, people are not allowed to take anything from the sound byte out of context to serve their own needs.
2. Incorporate this activity into team-building workshops and senior leadership retreats.

Case Study

This is a continuation of the story I began in the Background section of this activity. After two days of very intense discourse with a group of thirty-six professors from around the world on the nature of stories, complexity theory, and the relationship between the two, Theodore asked us to tame our racing minds and listen with all of our faculties. He had spent the night going through tapes of the last two days and had selected a three-minute sound byte of Professor David Boje being questioned about his development as a writer. David began to answer the question in an impersonal manner by enumerating various thinkers who have had an impact on him. The questions were part of a Socratic Circle wherein David and two other people were asked to clarify their ideas about the nature of stories. Through pointed questions and no interaction with each other or with the group at large who were watching the process, David and the other two people tried to reveal the basis for the thoughts and cherished assumptions about the nature of stories they hold. In this clip, the person playing Socrates pressed David to move beyond his impersonal analysis and speak about his personal experiences.

The group agreed to participate in the exercise, but there were undertones of grumbling among some people. We had just had an intense discussion about writing a book from the proceedings of the conference and people's minds were still wrapped around all of the details and concerns of undertaking the project. Although we had agreed to not complete the conversation about the book, as a whole, the group was not prepared for the listening experience created by Theodore's exercise.

We listened to the sound byte three times, and each time new things surfaced. There was a noticeable difference between how people connected to what they were hearing. One person was extremely analytical in his observations, unpacking bits and pieces of David's narrative. By attending to the same pieces each time, he explored greater levels of details. Others in the group picked up on emotions in David's voice. Some people discovered nuggets of meaning that surprised even David, but when queried about these, David agreed that these observations were on target. He was amazed that they had picked up on these things.

I had a very strange experience. I was quiet during the first two rounds of listening and discussing. I was fascinated by people's observations and remained in a listening mode during the discussions. While we were listening to the recording for the third time, I had a powerful and visceral reaction to what I heard. At one point in the recording, David responds to the interviewer with the word, "writing," followed by a long, awkward pause. I heard so much in that one word. When the recording was done, my heart was pounding and I had to share what I had heard. For a split second it was as if I heard not only the voice of David but the voice of other people in the room that David was embodying. As captured and transcribed from a recording here is what I said:

> "I felt my heart-palpitating … you said, *Writing! Writing!* You *answered* the question. The story was *completely* there, present in that moment, in its fullness, and then I think there was a mirroring of the energy of the group … there was a collective story that I felt emerge of Ph.D. students and scholars, and then this narrowing and this molding, and this pushing into a tunnel of, well, give this a voice, give what others of us are feeling, and yes, you had a thread of your own story and it was very real and genuine and was your point of view, but there was this polyphonic reality of what everyone else was feeling, and you were molded and guided and pushed to give that a voice and that was very interesting, and dangerous, and sacred, and wonderful, and mysterious, about the questioning and the facilitation and how group dynamics press on one another, I was really just moved."

There was pain, anger, frustration, desperation, assertion, determination, and hope wrapped up in that one word. David was describing how his time as a graduate student had destroyed him as a writer. My experience was strange because I felt like David was speaking for others as well as himself, and that's the way I heard it.

Three Channels

Three Channels

Background

I was standing around a company's coffee room a few minutes before I was supposed to facilitate a half-day workshop on active listening. I had been working with the senior managers of this company for six months. We had made some strides in improving communication between all the layers of management, but something was missing and I couldn't put my finger on it. As I sipped my coffee I listened to people's conversations. For a split moment, I became an unobserved observer and had one of those rare lucid moments when an epiphany strikes like a lightning bolt out of nowhere. In one conversation, a person's eyes were glazing over as he tried to take in all of the information. In another conversation, one person was paying attention to the information, but she was oblivious to the underlying emotions. And in a third conversation, I watched a person's unspoken intentions influencing an exchange. Between the lines of content and emotions, there was another source of information. I broke out of my reverie and walked into my session with a new untried activity, convinced I had something special. My gamble did not disappoint either me or the participants.

Facilitation Level
Difficult

Objectives
1. Develop stronger active listening skills by capturing and deciphering three channels of information.
2. Synthesize information from multiple channels to draw conclusions and guide communications with others.
3. Connect with others on a deeper and more fundamental level.

Materials
- None

Time
Forty-five minutes

Directions

1. Spend ten minutes talking about the three channels of information (content, emotions, and intentions—see the Tips section below for explanations and guidelines).

2. Ask for a volunteer to share a problem he or she is encountering at work or in his or her personal life. Tell the person to be prepared to speak for seven to ten minutes.

3. Divide people into three groups. Assign each group one channel of information (content, emotions, or intentions).

4. Let the volunteer share his or her story without any interruptions or questions.

5. Query each group to recount the information they obtained.

6. Debrief the group.

Debriefing

- When debriefing, query one channel at a time. Let each person in that group list one observation. Do a round robin until all the members of the group have exhausted their lists of observations. Verify the completeness of their information with the speaker before moving on to the next channel. After you have collected everyone's observations, offer some of your own. People will be fascinated by the gut channel, so this is a good time to answer more of their questions. Applaud their successes and allow participants to coach one another.

- Give the speaker an opportunity to respond to people's observations. Respect the speaker. He will be more vulnerable than he realizes. It's not unlikely that some of the observations will surprise him and maybe even hit a chord. There is a high degree of trust and reflective sensitivity created by this activity. So even if the speaker is surprised, it is very unlikely that he will feel threatened by the observations that surface. Anyone who volunteers to be a speaker is on some level ready and willing to expose himself.

- Steer the debriefing discussion away from solving the speaker's problem. If people have similar stories to share that's fine. Make time for this sort of discovery. Solving the speaker's problem is not the purpose of the activity and it will take people out of the "active listening" frame of reference.

- *How does breaking communication down into three channels contribute to active listening?* There is so much information we are decoding and interpreting all of the time. Active listening is the most critical and difficult communication skill to master. We know all of the things we do when we are not listening actively, but this activity helps people to experientially discover what it takes to listen actively. Focusing on one channel at a time heightens our awareness. The information is amplified, and we learn to become conscious of how we are forming impressions. It's important to understand how these channels interact with one another. Unless we practice active listening by breaking it down into observable components, we will never become mindful of our blind spots.

- *Is one channel more important than another?* All of the channels of information are important. We are naturally better at attending to some channels more than others. We need to recognize our listening strengths and weaknesses. By and large, listening to the gut is the toughest for people. Even though we are forming theories about what we hear and what it means, we do it unconsciously. Active listening helps us trace the disparate pieces of information we connect in our minds to derive our interpretations. We become reflective in the moment and synthesize current information with previous information. The gut enables us to enter a dialogue with a person. It guides us in a collaborative process of discovery with the speaker. When we synthesize what we are hearing in the moment with what we already know or think, communication takes on a deeper meaning. We move from superficial exchanges that appear rational on the surface, but which are saturated with all kinds of other information, to soulful listening. Breaking information into three channels is an excellent way to conceptualize the listening process. Listening can be further subdivided into additional sources of information; however, this is neither necessary nor beneficial. Active listening connects us to others and ourselves in a deeper and more fundamental way.

Variations
- Perform the activity in groups of four with one speaker and three listeners (one for each channel of information). Let groups debrief themselves and then do a large group debriefing.
- Run the activity once as a large group to model it and then break people into groups of four to run it on their own.
- Ask people to self-elect what channel of information they have the hardest time attending to. If you have noticed that someone struggles with one channel of information, suggest that she try listening to it.
- Do the activity in pairs. Have one person try to listen to all three channels of information. The listener goes through and details information for each channel and verifies it with his partners. Switch roles when done. People will need some practice before they will be able to do this variation.

Tips

- This activity will take some setup. Spend ten minutes discussing people's ideas about active listening. Then spend another five to ten minutes walking them through the three channels of information. I like to draw a picture of a person and label the channels as I go along:

  Head Channel (content)—the details and data of what is being communicated.

  Heart Channel (emotions)—the underlying emotions being expressed.

  Gut Channel (intentions)—the unspoken intentions of the speaker.

- I've also used short video clips to point out the channels of information. People understand the first two channels of information. These are obvious. Ask the group to explain how they pick up information from the heart channel. You want them to recognize all of the verbal and non-verbal ways this information is transmitted. The third channel of information, even with a good explanation, will be obtuse to people until they go through the activity at least once. The gut assimilates information from the first two channels and adds any background information or assumptions a listener has about the speaker. It amounts to guesswork. When you listen to the gut channel, you are crafting theories about why the person is sharing this information with you and trying to discern what else it might mean to the speaker, even when he is not consciously trying to communicate it. The more interpersonal experience you have with this person and the more stories you know about the person, the more accurate your gut read will be. Its okay for people to be uncomfortable and confused about what they are supposed to do to pick up information from the gut channel. Insist that you will not be able to clarify their questions until they try the activity. More detail-oriented people will be frustrated and angry with your ambiguity, but just live with it. Don't try to resolve the tension.

- Don't facilitate this activity without first trying it yourself. This is a great activity to do on your own, since it will increase your skills as facilitator by strengthening your active listening skills.

- If you do this in a large group, ask people to challenge themselves by listening to a channel of information that is difficult for them. If I will not be violating a personal boundary, I will assign people to channels that I think will challenge them.

- Make sure you assign at least one person to your gut channel group who has demonstrated this ability earlier in your session.

- Stick to speakers talking about personal or work-related problems. This is guaranteed to yield a rich flow of information on all of the channels.

- It's imperative that you be capable of listening to all the channels of information simultaneously. Make sure you have plenty of energy when you do this activity—it's exhausting. Regardless of how long it takes to do this activity, I suggest taking a break immediately following it. When you reconvene the group, it's a good time to engage them in a brief period of passive learning (short lecture, self-paced activity, video, or some lighthearted storytelling).

- When you add to the group's observations, be animated. I will stand up and provide an instant replay of the speaker's words and body language.

- Working with the gut channel requires you to have a good running mental log of key actions, words, and stories shared by the speaker. You will use these when you synthesize information being communicated by the speaker with everything you know about the speaker. The group needs to see how you come to your conclusions. Its okay if people listening to the gut cannot articulate all of the things that they have used to come up with their theories, but you must be able to list all of the pieces of information and explain how you have combined them to draw your conclusion. Help people understand that reading the gut channel demands humility and flexibility. It's not about being right; it's about forming some ideas and probing further. Active listening promotes dialogue and collaboration between speakers and listeners.

Applications

1. Build this activity as a key component of almost any program, especially customer service, sales, and supervisor training.

2. Establish this practice of active listening during workshops, retreats, and other professional development activities; then use this technique to facilitate conflict resolution.

3. Whenever a problem is going to be presented during any type of meeting, ask the group to share its observations of the three channels of information before moving into any other phase of the discussion.

Case Study

Jack's hand shot up to volunteer to be the speaker for the activity. Jack, who was a young retired colonel in the army, had been a natural leader all week. There was excellent chemistry in the group, and people appreciated Jack's comments and thoughts. Although he was an active participant, Jack did not share much personal information. This contributed to creating an aura of mystery and even personal power around him. Prior to the activity, we had had a rousing discussion on active listening. People had an excellent intellectual grasp of the concept. The group was eager to try the activity, although no one had a clue as to what I meant by the gut channel. Jack stood up and put his hands behind his back as if he was preparing to give a briefing to commanding officers and began to tell us his story. It was a classic story of being caught in the middle between senior-level executives he could exert minimal influence on and staff that were dependent on him to understand and represent their needs. Like a good soldier, he was forced to toe the line, despite the fact that he disagreed with what he was being asked to do. As an IT director, Jack needed to execute strategies and enact policies, practices, and procedures he did not agree with. He presented a well-oiled, rational account of his current situation. His words were objective, his emotions were riddled with strains of frustration and repressed passion for his staff's needs, circumvented with logical analyses and recommendations. And through it all he was striving for something that was beyond his reach, the freedom to act in the best interests of others unconstrained by duties imposed by forces out of his control. There was a moment of silence when he was done. People finished compiling their observations, and we began the debriefing process. We started with the head channel. Jack's words were easy to follow. His speech was organized, deliberate, and thorough. Next we moved to the heart channel. As a group, with some probing on my part and occasional reenactment of Jack's story, we unearthed a slew of subtle emotions all expressed through visible, easily observable actions. One example led to another. Jack was stunned as he listened to people. He was convinced that whatever emotion he had was buried deep within him and out of view from others. So when people picked up on his emotions and provided him with concrete examples of gestures, eye and head movements, and vocal variations to support their conclusions, he didn't know what to think. Then we dropped the bomb. Once we started discussing the gut channel, Jack, who had been standing up until this point, grabbed a chair and sat down. People combined facts with emotions and merged them with comments, stories, and observations from things they had remembered he had shared with the group earlier in the week. The insights were right on target, and Jack confirmed each one. Jack confided with the group and delved deeper into many of the "gut" theories people had put forward. People were blown away by the activity, overwhelmed by how exhausting active listening really is, but invigorated by its powerful possibilities. I let everyone go home early that day.

Storytelling Energizers

Storytelling Energizers

This chapter deals with the mechanics of storytelling. It begins with some tips and techniques for telling stories. Next the chapter offers ideas on how to select a story. The concepts of indexing explored in Chapter 2 and the Introduction to Part Two are re-examined. The chapter ends with ten storytelling exercises that are easy and fun to do and that are guaranteed to energize any group.

How to Tell a Story

There is an art to telling a story. It's important to remember that everyone has a different personality. Your personality will influence your storytelling style. There is no "right" way to tell a story. I am reminded of what a funny scene a colleague of mine and I must make when we tell stories together. We often tell stories to children in English and Spanish. I'll start to tell the story in English and he translates it into Spanish. I become very excited. I jump around the room, flapping my arms up and down. My eyes grow large, and my voice bellows with energy. My colleague, on the other hand, is calm. He barely moves and he has one of those soft, deep, mellow voices. He is subtler but just as effective, if not more so. So what makes us effective?

Whatever your personality, there are three essential aspects to telling a story:

1. A desire to connect
2. Sensitivity to the moods, needs, and desires of a group
3. Reliving the story as you tell it

A Desire to Connect

You have to want to communicate. Whether you are introverted or extroverted doesn't matter. In Part One of the book, we learned how stories create an environment and help people to bind and bond with one another. When you tell a story, focus on your desire to reach out. Sharing a story is a genuine response. It's intimate. Imagine a person who is either sad or depressed. Now imagine a special conversation with a loved one. What's different between the two images? Have you ever noticed how difficult it is for a person who is depressed to communicate? He or she will not want to make eye contact, and you have to work hard to get any response at all, whereas an intimate conversation with a loved one is filled with stories. You have so much you want to share. Think of storytelling, whatever the venue or purpose, as an intimate conversation. When you have something you want to communicate, using a story will have the greatest impact.

Sensitivity to the Moods, Needs, and Desires of the Group

The moods, needs, and desires of a group dictate when to tell a story and what story to tell. Have you ever told a joke and gotten no response? Or made an excellent comment or point that went unheard because you picked the wrong time to voice it? As a storyteller you must learn how to tune in to the dynamics of a group. Stories require active listening. Actively listening to a group is more difficult because there are more people you need to be aware of. Here are nine ideas to get you started:

1. *Answer people's questions with a story.* Are people asking similar questions? Questions are good. It means people are thinking. Now your job as a facilitator is to transport people into a reflective space. Telling a story or finding someone in the group to share one will enrich the discussion. Normally when we have a question we seek to alleviate the uncertainty caused by it. We want an answer. This, however, is not always in our best interest. As the great romantic poet Rainer Maria Rilke wrote in a letter to a young man, "Learn to love the questions." Answering a question with a story encourages people to sit with them and mull them over in new ways. Stories encourage self and community discovery. The questions become building blocks. Each question acts as a new thread to be woven into a intricate tapestry of knowledge and wisdom. When you use a story, be sure to get people to draw parallels between the story told and the questions they are asking. If people become stuck, offer some analysis and insights.

2. *Elicit stories from the group.* Are there common themes to the comments people are making? Comments made during group discussions tend to cluster around themes. Rather than just collecting bullets on flip charts, elicit stories from the group and use them as organizing devices. Ask people to be specific and give examples. They will end up sharing personal experiences in the form of stories. These are your gateway to great insights. Synthesize people's experiences to make new points and to reinforce previous ones. Stories are great tools when you have lots of complex information. You can manipulate stories to encode and decode information far more efficiently than you can other forms of information. Eliciting stories during group discussion will help you tie people's comments together in a meaningful way that they are likely to remember.

3. *Use a metaphor or analogy.* Do people need an idea or concept to be illustrated? Help people to visualize the idea or concept you are trying to explain by applying a metaphor or analogy from another domain. When we draw an example from an area people are familiar with, it establishes a linkage of learning to the new information we are introducing. These analogies and metaphors acting as stories allow us to drop people into mental simulators that fabricate new constructs. After you provide one, ask people to think of another one. This solidifies the concept for them and gives them confidence. It also allows you to make sure they have grasped the concept.

4. *Tell a story to change the group's energy.* What is the group's energy? There are natural ebbs and flows. A story can stimulate and revitalize a group. Likewise, stories can help a group relax and become centered. Stories are wonderful tools for creating an environment. Be sure to develop a large repertoire of stories. These do not have to be long in order to be effective, nor do they even have to be told by you. Your main challenge as a facilitator is to begin to become cognizant of subtle shifts in the group. It is your job to maintain the most optimal environment. Use stories to redirect people and adjust the group's energy.

5. *Tell a story with your voice and body language.* What are people saying with their body language? When you tell a story, match the tone and body language of individuals in the group. People will become more aware of what they are saying through their bodies and begin to modify their body language. As they do so, there will be subtle shifts in their perceptions and emotions.

6. *Validate and transform emotions with a story.* Are there underlying emotions? Tell a story that mirrors the emotions you sense in the group in a non-didactic and non-patronizing way. This validates unspoken emotions and allows people to move past them. Once negative feelings are acknowledged, they can be examined safely through the story and even transformed into more positive ones. Stories are multi-sensory vehicles of communication. We can use them to mirror what we observe in the group. For example, if a group is feeling vulnerable after a discussion or workshop, share a story that you know will resonate with those feelings of vulnerability. Be careful, as this can be dangerous territory. As with any technique, we must be mindful not to abuse it. When you mirror, people check your intentions. If gaining power and control of people is your motivation, stay clear of these techniques. Authenticity and genuine care for people's well-being should be at the forefront of our minds.

7. *Tell a story to change people's perspective.* Has the group become stuck? Stories can be used as tools to encourage thinking. A group becomes stuck when it is unable to imagine other possibilities. The psychologist James Hillman talks about getting stuck in our habits of thought and behavior. These are the places we frequent and habituate. When we become locked into one story, the best way to escape its gravitational pull is to introduce another one that moves our imaginations in new ways. Stories can be rich sources of irony and paradox. These, in turn, challenge a group's current thinking and can lead them in new directions.

8. *Use people's stories to build role plays on the fly.* Are people sharing similar types of experiences? As people share their experiences, others may respond with similar stories of their own. These stories can be revisited to examine alternative behaviors by turning them into role plays. Ask people for permission to use their stories as role plays for the group. Elicit as many details about the situation or person to help re-create the story as a role play in the most compelling fashion possible. This helps everyone to enter the story and work with it as a virtual simulator. It also gives the teller an opportunity to dive deeper into his or her past experience and by doing so gain new insights. Listeners will also have an opportunity to scan their experiences for corresponding elements. The assignment of roles in the role play can be done in a variety of ways depending on the situation and the nature of the role play. Use your judgment. When in doubt you can always ask the tellers to play themselves in the role play and you can take on one of the key roles if there is more than one. One of the more challenging aspects of turning stories into role plays is knowing when to freeze the role play to point out learning, ask for suggestions from the group, or allow the group to process what is occurring. In general, thirty seconds of role play can yield up to fifteen minutes of group processing. Some examples of the types of discussion you can lead following a role play include asking people to analyze how their own stories would have been different if they adopted any of the strategies identified by the group and what people will try differently when they find themselves in a similar situation in the future.

9. *Use a joke or tangent.* Has the group become too analytical? Jokes are a great tool for getting people to be less analytical. Jokes are like little epiphanies. A joke is funny because the punch line is unexpected. It hits us as a surprise. Telling a joke or leaving the subject at hand to go off on a tangent will help a group become less analytical and more creative.

Reliving the Story as You Retell It

Stories are in danger of becoming static and ineffectual if they are memorized like a script. Remembering a story involves reliving the details as you tell it. Since stories are an oral tradition, many of the details change over time. When I tell a story, I always try to introduce new details that are relevant to the group I am telling it to. Groups respond well to story tailoring. It makes the story special and increases the group's interest, attention, participation, and retention.

Techniques for Telling Stories

I know I am telling a story well when I am surprised by what the characters say and by the events in the story as they unfold. Reliving a story as you tell it makes it easier to keep a large catalogue of indexed stories in your mind. The stories are compressed, but they expand to their full size once you start to tell them. The story seems more real and engaging to the audience, as well as to the teller. For the teller, the story takes on new shades of meaning and enables him or her to discover new insights. Here are some techniques for telling a story well (this material is also available on the accompanying CD-ROM):

1. Voice. Your voice brings a story alive. Think of your voice as an instrument. Instruments are played with dynamics (i.e., sometimes loud, sometimes soft).

- Animate the stories you tell by varying the pitch, tone, and volume of your voice.
- Use your voice to guide listeners. Emphasize key words, phrases, or details.
- Change your voice to represent characters in your story.
- Insert brief pauses and other rhythmical speech variations.

2. Repetition. Stories are filled with repetition. These patterns help listeners remember a story and reflect on it later. As a result of repetition, listeners are more actively involved because they are anticipating a recurring theme or pattern.

- Repeat descriptive details.
- Select vivid and multi-sensorial words and reuse them throughout your story.
- Give listeners a vocal or bodily cue before repeating a pattern.

3. Participation. Stories are more engaging when people participate. When you tell a story, do everything you can to involve your audience. The result? People will listen more carefully and get more out of the story.

- Customize the details of your story to fit the group it is being told to.

- Allow listeners to fill in descriptive, non-critical details of a story.
- In your story, use the names, facts, and characteristics of individuals in the group.
- Include in the story comments individuals have made during the session.
- Weave recent events into your stories.
- Incorporate repetitive elements and have your listeners fill them in.
- Use rhetorical questions.

4. Body language. A story is told with the voice and the body. Have you ever watched a good mime? Body language can communicate more than words.

- Make eye contact with individuals.
- Develop special gestures and postures for story situations and characters.
- Act out parts of the story.
- Use props.
- Move around the room as you tell the story.

It may seem as if this is a lot to be aware of when telling a story, but these things happen naturally when you are connected to the story and to the people you are telling it to.

How to Select a Story

People ask me all the time, "How do I select an effective story for my learning event?" I cannot claim there is an exact science to the process, but I have developed some guidelines to help people determine what kinds of stories are more appropriate than others given certain environmental variables.

Selecting a Story

Use the matrix on the next page to determine what type of story to select. There are three steps to the process. First, select a word from the row titled "1. Size," which best describes the size of group you intend to select a story for. Second, select a word from the row titled, "2. Intention." Last, select a word from the row titled, "3. Trigger." At the bottom of each column there is a number indicating a value. Add up the values of your choices using the values listed at the bottom of each column to obtain your overall score.

	Intimate	Small	Meeting	Presentation
1. Size "How many people will hear your story?"	Usually a conversation involving two people, the nature of the exchange is personal	Several people who share good relationships with one another	More formal setting, there is structure to the group interactions, people may or may not know one another well or have good relationships	Very formal setting, usually large group
	Connect	**Teach**	**Transfer**	**Entertain**
2. Intention "Why do you need to select a story?"	You need to build stronger relationships and a bond with your listeners	You need to elucidate, explain, or help others conceptualize new ideas or concepts	You need to communicate key pieces of information	You need to break the ice, empower yourself as a speaker, or make people laugh
	Listen	**Insight**	**Reaction**	**Plant**
3. Trigger "What is prompting you to select a story?"	You want to hear what a person is thinking or feeling so you share a personal story to create an opportunity for reciprocity	You need to share an epiphany or while you are listening you suddenly realize something new	You need to respond to another person's story or comment; you may also be responding to group dynamics	You need to deliver a very specific message or invoke a specific mood
	Column Value = 1	**Column Value = 2**	**Column Value = 3**	**Column Value = 4**

Score	What Kind of Story to Select
3 to 6	Personal Story
6 to 9	Other People's Personal Stories
9 to 12	Stories from Other Domains

There is some overlap between the categories' scores to account for situations that naturally could fall into either one. This is meant to be a guideline. You may end up with a score of 12 and decide that selecting a personal story is still the best option. As a general rule, I place a higher value on personal stories; however, they are not always appropriate.

Personal Stories run the gamut from very recent experiences to experiences deep in our pasts. There is often a quality of vulnerability associated with sharing a personal story, especially one from our past. We often relate personal stories in the form of a collage. Stories that are well-indexed in our minds will be tightly interwoven with one another, and we may feel the desire to share a series of linked stories. The key to selecting stories is having plenty to choose from. While it is possible to get a lot of mileage out of a few stories and reuse them in a variety of settings, this is not optimal. Reviewing our categories of stories, we know personal stories require a rich index. These are your most important ones. If you find yourself coming up short on personal stories to share, then you need to spend more time reflecting on them. Another good source of personal stories are recent experiences, since they are current in our minds. Be aware of sharing a story to simply vent or boast. Stories used in a self-serving fashion do not resonate well with others. They have little impact and communication potential.

Other People's Personal Stories may come from ones they have shared with us. They can also be events we have observed. The major defining characteristic of these stories is that they describe things that have not happened to us. For sharing other people's personal stories, recent experiences are also effective. If we have recently heard another person's story, we are likely to remember it. This story can be used when we do not want to share a personal one or when it is inappropriate to do so. Stories that really strike us stay with us. We are bound to have a collection of stories we have heard from others that are not recent ones. They need to be well-indexed along with our personal ones.

Stories from Other Domains is the last category of stories. Stories from other domains may come from anywhere. Some good examples are books, movies, history, or science. That is not an exhaustive list, but gives you the sense that these are stories drawn from lots of different disciplines.

Becoming comfortable with extemporaneously selecting an effective story to tell requires experience and a very rich index of stories. In the Introduction to Part Two and in Chapter 2 we discussed the important role of indexing. Our index is how we find stories and how we link them together and associate them with whatever information we are processing in the moment. Knowing what story in the moment will resonate with a group and elicit stories from them requires strong listening and observation skills (see the discussion of the Core in Chapter 2).

Story Energizers

Here are ten of my favorite storytelling exercises. I use these any time I need to energize a group. These are intended to be short exercises. They provide people with a break from what they are doing, while helping them to strengthen critical communication skills of extemporaneous creativity. If I am facilitating an all-day workshop, afternoons are a perfect time to insert one of these exercises. People get an opportunity to exercise their storytelling skills while having some fun.

Many of these exercises do not need to have a clear end. In other words, not everyone in the group needs to do the exercise in order for it to be effective and reinvigorate a group. Run an exercise long enough to get people recharged. You will find that observers have just as much fun as participants. If you are running a multi-day event or the group you are doing these exercises with meets on a regular basis, you can return to an exercise and pick up where you left off and give other people a chance to participate. I like this sort of continuity because it provides excitement for people. They look forward to the exercise and have a good time trying to outdo each other.

Story Energizer	Objective
1. Grab Bag	Use random objects to stimulate impromptu storytelling.
2. Start Finish Start	Create an improvised story as a group.
3. Stone Soup	Explore the stories connected to common objects.
4. I Remember When . . .	Use "key moments of life" and fictitious events to trigger stories.
5. Musical Story	Use a piece of music to stimulate people to tell a story.
6. Match Maker	Transform people's fun facts into a storytelling game.
7. If I Were . . .	Place people in contrived situations to prompt zany stories.
8. Genie in a Bottle	Imagine the consequences of a fulfilled wish and tell a story about it.
9. Story Interrupts	Discover how stories are present in conversations all the time.
10. Reverse Plots	Imagine alternative scenarios to well-known movies.

1. Grab Bag

Use random objects to stimulate impromptu storytelling.
Time Required: Three minutes to set up the exercise, two minutes per person

- Create a bag filled with random objects (anything works, e.g., paperweight, pens, toys, etc.). Be wacky but use good judgment. To spice things up, try throwing in an object that is representative of the organization.

- Have people select an object. If it's a small group, have everyone select an object from the bag; otherwise determine how much time you want the exercise to take and ask for an appropriate number of volunteers.

- Instruct people they have two minutes to think of a story about their objects. It doesn't matter if it's a real story from their experience or a made-up story. There is no need to provide too much guidance—let people have fun with it.

2. Start Finish Start

Create an improvised story as a group.
Time Required: Ten minutes

- If possible, have people sit in a circle. Inform them that they will be working as a group to make up a story on the spot in "real time." This exercise works equally well with a small group (five person minimum) or with large groups.

For large groups, ask for volunteers and arrange a circle of chairs in the front of the room, or if the room does not permit it, have people stay where they are.

- Start a story, "Once upon a time. . . ." Fill in the first sentence or two. I try to incorporate subjects and details relevant to the group, but it's not necessary. Let the story go where it will. Each person adds to the story by filling in a few sentences and then handing it off to the next person. Continue this way one or two times around the circle. You can be the designated story-ender or randomly inform a participant that he or she must finish the story.

3. Stone Soup
Explore the stories connected to common objects.
Time Required: Three minutes per object, two-minute debriefing at the end

- Call on a participant to point to any object in the room. It can be anything, so don't worry about how mundane the object might be. That's part of the beauty of this exercise.

- Ask for three volunteers to act as storytellers. One must offer a story explaining where the object came from, the second volunteer must offer a story of how it came into being, and the third must offer a story of how the object got into the room.

- After the stories are finished, see whether anyone else in the group has any other story to add.

- Conduct a mini debriefing at the end of the exercise. People are surprised at how many interconnected dependencies and stories there are behind a simple day-to-day object that we tend to take for granted. This insight can be applied to many organizational and interpersonal situations.

4. I Remember When . . .
Use "key moments of life" and fictitious events to trigger stories.
Time Required: Two minutes per person

- Prepare a stack of index cards with "I remember when. . ." phrases that reference both real-life events and fictitious ones. Here are some examples to get you started:

Real Events. . .
  I remember when I took my first trip to a foreign country.
  I remember when I bought my first car.

I remember when I went on my first date.

I remember when I had my first job interview.

Fictitious Events . . .

I remember when I won my first grand-prix racing event.

I remember when I walked on the moon.

I remember when I had dinner with [insert famous person of your choice].

I remember when I starred in my first block-buster movie.

(*Note:* Sometimes it's fun to let the participants come up with the phrases).

- If everyone will not be doing the exercise, ask for volunteers. Have people select an index card at random. Give them a minute to prepare their stories.

5. Musical Story

Use a piece of music to stimulate people to tell a story.
Time Required: Four minutes per piece of music

- Select some pieces of music to play. It's best to have the music queued up ahead of time.
- Play a piece of music for one or two minutes and then ask for volunteers to share a story invoked by the music. It can either be a real story (e.g., perhaps a memory evoked by the music) or it can be a story they make up based on how the music stirs their emotions and imaginations.

6. Match Maker

Transform people's fun facts intro a storytelling game.
Time Required: Four minutes per fun fact

- Have everyone write down a fun or interesting personal fact that no one in the group knows.
- Draw a card at random and read the fact out loud. Ask the group to guess who this fun fact belongs to. Get three nominations.
- Have three nominees stand up and take turns telling a story about the fun fact.
- After all of the nominees have told their stories, ask the group to vote on whether they think the nominee is the person or not. Tally the votes.
- When the voting is complete, ask the person to whom the fun fact belongs to reveal him- or herself to the group. Give the person a chance to tell his or her story.

7. If I Were . . .

Place people in contrived situations to prompt zany stories.
Time Required: Three minutes per phrase

- Write down a list of "If I were . . ." phrases on index cards. Here are a few ideas to get you started:
  - If I were King for a day . . .
  - If I were the ocean . . .
  - If I were the smartest person in the world . . .
  - If I were a computer . . .
  - If I were a Martian . . .
- Ask a volunteer to select a card at random and complete the sentence. Then ask the person to pick a person to tell a story that illustrates the completed phrase.

8. Genie in a Bottle

Have people imagine the consequences of a fulfilled wish and tell a story about it.
Time Required: Two minutes per wish plus one minute to set up the exercise

- Ask for a volunteer without telling the person what he or she will be doing, but assure the person it is safe, fun, and entertaining.
- Give the rest of the people in the group index cards. Tell them a genie has been freed from his bottle and will grant them any wish. They should write their wishes on their index cards.
- Collect the index cards and put them in a bag. Let the volunteer draw a card at random. Instruct him that he must tell a story about how his life is different as a result of this fulfilled wish. When the volunteer has finished, let him pick another person who must draw a card and tell a story. Repeat the sequence as many times as you want.

9. Story Interrupts

Discover how stories are present in conversations all the time.
Time Required: Five to seven minutes per topic plus three minutes to set up the exercise the first time

- Place five chairs in a circle at the front of the room.
- Ask for four volunteers to join you for a conversation. Explain that this will be a discussion composed completely of stories. Brainstorm some discussion topics with the group. Steer the group toward topics that are likely to trigger

lots of personal stories. For example, "My high school years, my college years, time with my best friends," etc.

- Invite the volunteers to sit down in the chairs. Inform them that you will start the conversation by sharing a story. The moment anyone in conversation remembers a story that is triggered by the one you are telling, ask the person to raise his or her hand and keep it raised until you are finished. When you finish your story, if there is more than one person with his or her hand raised, select one to tell his or her story. Continue until you run out of stories or until you reach your desired time limit for the discussion.

10. Reverse Plots
Imagine alternative scenarios to well-known movies.
Time Required: Ten minutes per movie

- Brainstorm a list of well-known movies with the group. Identify a movie that everyone knows. If there are one or two people unfamiliar with the movie, ask someone to give a brief synopsis of the movie.
- Ask someone to suggest a major change to the movie's plot.
- Lead a group discussion of how this proposed change would alter the story and its characters.

The Power of Stories
Is in the Listening*

The challenges of managing people and processes are mitigated by the power of stories. Communication is the foundation for managing, and stories are one of the best ways to understand the mechanisms of effective communication. Our pursuit of better management practices can be achieved if we learn to listen actively to the stories around us and if we use these stories to negotiate our differences.

Do you ever feel that you are not heard or understood? It's no surprise that our relationships at work and at home are often riddled with problems. We do a horrible job of listening to each other. To make matters worse, we do not treat our experiences with circumspection; therefore we fail to garner insights and learning from them. We stumble along oblivious to other people's perspectives and unaware of what experiences have contributed to the development of the perceptual filters that color each person's world view. If it were just our own world view, we might not care, but this inaccessible, foggy filter also guides the behavior affecting others.

The following short story provides a glimpse of the problems that occur when we become engrossed in our own perceptions:

The Train Story . . .

Four travelers shared a train compartment: a beautiful young woman, the young woman's grandmother, a distinguished general, and a young officer. As the train sped along at night, the lights in the compartment suddenly turned off. In the darkness two distinct sounds could be heard from the compartment—the sound of a wet juicy kiss and the sound of a hand

---

*Parts of this article have been adapted and reprinted from *Stories at Work: Using Stories to Improve Communications and Build Relationships.* Terrence L. Gargiulo. Copyright © 2006 by Praeger Publishers. Reproduced with permission of Greenwood Publishing Group, Inc., Westport, CT.

slapping the side of a face. When the lights turned back on, the faces of the travelers told a story. The young woman's face was red from embarrassment. She was mortified to think that the young man had kissed her in the dark. She was very thankful that she was traveling with her grandmother, who slapped the young man. The grandmother's hands were clenched in fists of rage and she was fuming. She could not believe that the general would try to take advantage of her granddaughter, but she was glad she had taught her granddaughter to never let a man touch her without permission. Her granddaughter had done the right thing to slap that dirty old man. The veins in the general's neck were bulging. He was furious. He had tried to teach the young officer about respect and discipline. The general couldn't believe that the young whippersnapper had kissed the beautiful woman, who then mistakenly had slapped the general. The young man was grinning from ear to ear. He couldn't believe his good fortune. How often do you get to kiss a beautiful young woman and slap your boss at the same time?

Everyone is mixed up in this story except for our friend, the young officer. Emotions run high and the characters are operating literally and figuratively in the dark. Isn't this story representative of how we are guilty of acting sometimes? We seldom know the "real story" behind someone's feelings, beliefs, or actions. Worse yet, we do not make the effort to discover their stories. Convinced of our opinions, we prefer to keep our mental model of the world neat and orderly by staying focused on our perspectives, rather than entertaining another point of view. While these natural proclivities of our minds are assets intended by evolution to equip our species with the ability to act independently and decisively, they are also liabilities when it comes to relationships. When we actively listen to other people's stories, we do not need to abandon our ideas; instead we can enter a new frame of reference by reconstituting the story being shared with us in our minds and hearts. Stories allow us to move in and out of different frames of reference. We are, in essence, "standing in someone else's shoes."

Management has come to mean control to many people. If we cannot control something or someone, how can we manage it? Relationships cannot be controlled. We have to learn how to get in pace with each other, and we have to work at it. Yet managing is all about relationships, and relationships depend on open lines of communications. We cannot enact a policy to ensure people take the time and effort to hear one another. We must model these behaviors and invest a tremendous amount of energy and patience into sustaining these fragile conduits. Stories turn out to be a great tool to do this.

Hearing someone else's story may not change our perspective, but it opens up dialogue and increases the chance of a mutually satisfying resolution. While we may not become expert listeners overnight, stories help us understand another's perspective because they require active listening. Stories catapult our imaginations into new directions. Many of our habitual ways of looking at things can be altered by a story's capacity to engage us. Our connection to others and our understanding of their perspectives is deepened by a story's ability to inform us in ways that words by themselves cannot do.

I remember watching my father conduct orchestra rehearsals. He begins his first rehearsal with any orchestra by saying, "If I cannot speak to you with this baton, we're both in trouble!" And while my father said very little, he communicated a lot, and he listened intently. Even during the loudest section of music, when all of the instruments are playing *forte,* my father can isolate the sound of one violinist playing the wrong sharp or flat. Communicating with one another would be a lot easier if we all had such exceptional listening skills.

Before we move away from music, take a moment to consider why the same piece of music evokes different emotions in different people. Could it be that the emotive power of music is tied to people's memories, stories, and the associations they make? In this respect, stories and music are very similar. I am reminded of the wonderful cliché: *"A wise old owl lived in an oak; the more he saw, the less he spoke; the less he spoke, the more he heard. Why can't we all be like that wise old bird?"*

Stories have multiple threads. Stories do not grow old. However, our imaginations grow lazy. We need to challenge ourselves. Is it possible for us to find a new nugget of gold each time we hear or relay a story? Can we find an unturned rock, a new nuance? To do so, we must develop the capacity for active listening.

What we need is less doing and more listening. But the amount of each is a hard thing to quantify. The results are undeniable, but they somehow evade direct observation. Like a tree that changes color in the fall and loses its leaves in winter, the transformations are imperceptible on a daily basis, but when viewed from a seasonal perspective the results are staggering. Managing through stories built on the functional requirement of active listening is like our analogy of a tree.

Managing is an art of bringing our attention into the moment. Like the wise old owl, the more we strive to hear people's stories the more we will be able to manage by not managing. Put another way, as we listen to each other's stories it becomes possible to negotiate differences. More often than not, our conflicts are a function of not hearing and understanding one another. Spontaneous solutions and resolutions arise when we enter someone else's frame of reference. Sharing our stories generates vivid pictures for others because when we listen actively we bring our experiences to their telling. Therefore, a bridge of understanding is constructed between two or more people. Our greatest challenge as managers is to create an environment of genuine interest, trust, openness, and reciprocity where people willingly share their stories.

Sample Breakthrough Communication Skills Workshop Agendas

There are many different ways to combine the activities in this book to build your own workshop agendas. Here are some questions to guide you:

1. How many people will be in your workshop?
2. How much time do you have?
3. Will you work with these people in multiple sessions or is this a one-shot deal?
4. Can you fold these activities into an existing agenda?
5. Have people been introduced to how stories function and the story-based communication competency model?

Outlined below are three basic learning modules you can piece together to create your own workshops. Use these modules as a foundation for whatever you develop. For multi-day workshops, organize the rest of your workshop around activities connected with the competency model (See Chapter 2). There are two charts in the Introduction to Part Two of the book that will help you.

Module 1: Introduction to Stories

Exercise 1: Tell Me Who You Are

Materials
- Handout: "Nine Functions of Stories" (from the CD-ROM)
- Audio: "The Man with No Story" (from the CD-ROM)

Time
Twenty-five minutes for sharing, fifteen for debriefing

Directions
1. Have people pair off, if possible with someone they do not know.
2. Instruct one person from each pair to talk about himself or herself while the other sits and listens. The listener cannot ask any questions or say anything.
3. After ten minutes, have them switch roles.
4. Debrief the exercise.

Facilitator Notes
- This is an interesting exercise to watch. For one thing, many people dislike talking about themselves. They feel that they have very little to say and that their lives are not very interesting. Typically, people approach the exercise like an interview. They begin rattling off the facts of their lives (where they were born, raised, went to school, and worked). Before long they run out of things to say, but there is usually a lot of time left. Without realizing what they are doing, they begin telling stories. Suddenly time begins to compress, they realize they have a lot to say, and they become more animated. You can also observe a change in the listeners. Listeners lean forward and become more involved in what the person is saying.

- After the activity, get people to share their experiences and observations. See whether they can identify when they switched into a storytelling mode versus a fact-relating mode. Go around the room and have people give examples. Encourage them to draw parallels between the exercise and communication in general. See whether people can recall similar experiences, such as when they had trouble communicating or used a story.

Debriefing
Brainstorm people's ideas about what stories are. Explore people's thoughts on whether they believe stories are effective. Time permitting, I like to tell people the

story of "The Man with No Story." (Use the audio file on the CD-ROM, which is seven minutes in length.)

Exercise 2. Mini Interactive Lecture

Time
Twenty minutes

Directions
Walk people through the Nine Functions of Stories. Do so in an interactive lecture format. Be sure to provide lots of rich examples. Use the handout on the CD-ROM titled "The Nine Functions of Stories."

Module 2: Story-Based Communication Competency Tool (SCCT)

Time
Sixty minutes

Materials
- Copies of the SCCT for participants (these can be ordered from www.making stories.net or by calling (781) 894–4381). This includes self-development exercises for participants to try on their own.
- Handout titled "Story-Based Communication Competency Model" from the CD-ROM. (There are both color and black-and-white versions of the handout.)
- Flash file: animated graphic of the competency model from the CD-ROM

Directions
1. Administer the SCCT, which takes about twenty minutes. If you have not already administered the tool prior to the workshop (that is, as a 360-degree feedback tool), then with very little introduction ask people to fill it out.
2. Give a mini interactive lecture, which should take about fifteen minutes. Use the animated Flash file and handouts to discuss the story-based communication competency model.

Debriefing
Help people to understand their scores. Give people fifteen minutes to develop a personal action plan based on their results and to identify some self-development exercises they want to try from the SCCT booklet.

Module 3: Experiential Intro to the Story-Based Communication Competency Model

Time
Ninety minutes

Materials
- A copy of this book
- Handout: a blank Story Collage™ Form
- Handout: one of the Sample Story Collage™ forms from the CD-ROM. There are two to choose from.
- Handout: Sample Story Collage™ text from the CD-ROM. There are two to chose from.
- Audio sample segment for Take Three from the CD-ROM

The following activities give people a feel for key competencies for the three rings of the model, are easy to facilitate, and can be done within a relatively short time period.

1. Expand and Collapse gives a sample of the interaction ring.
2. Story Collage™ shows how to use the process ring.
3. Take Three gives the core.

Suggested Reading

Abrahams, Roger D. *African Folktales*. New York: Pantheon Books, 1983.

Armstrong, David M. *Managing by Storying Around: A New Method of Leadership*. New York: Doubleday, 1992.

Baldwin, Christina. *Storycatcher: Making Sense of Our Lives Through the Power and Practice of Story*. Novato, CA: New World Library, 2005.

Berman, Michael, and Brown, David. *The Power of Metaphor*. New York: Crown, 2001.

Boje, David. *Narrative Methods for Organizational & Communication Research*. London: Sage, 2001.

Boje, David. *Storytelling Organization: Story Escaping Narrative Prison*. London: Sage, 2007.

Brown, Juanita, and Isaacs, David. *The World Café: Shaping Our Futures Through Conversations That Matter*. San Francisco, CA: Berrett-Koehler, 2005.

Brown, John Seely, Denning, Stephen, Groh, Katalina,, and Prusak, Lawrence. *Storytelling in Organizations: Why Storytelling Is Transforming the 21st Century Organizations and Management*. Burlington, MA: Elsevier Butterworth-Heinemann, 2005.

Bushnaq, Inea. *Arab Folktales*. New York: Pantheon, 1986.

Calvino, Italo. *Italian Folktales*. San Diego, CA: Harcourt, Brace, Jovanovich, 1980. (translated by George Martin and originally published in 1956 by Giulio Einaudi editore, s.p.a.)

Campbell, Joseph. *The Power of Myth with Bill Moyers*. New York: Doubleday, 1988.

Canfield, Jack, and Miller, Jacqueline. *Heart at Work: Stories and Strategies for Building Self-Esteem and Reawakening the Soul at Work*. New York: McGraw-Hill, 1996.

Chinen, Allan B. *In the Ever After: Fairy Tales and the Second Half of Life*. Wilmette, IL: Chiron Publications, 1989.

Chinen, Allan B. *Once Upon a Midlife: Classic Stories and Mythic Tales to Illuminate the Middle Years*. New York: Tarcher/Putnam, 1992.

Clark, Evelyn. *Around the Corporate Campfire: How Great Leaders Use Stories to Inspire Success*. Sevierville, TN: Insight, 2004.

Collins, R., & Cooper, P.J. *The Power of Story: Teaching Through Storytelling*. Boston, MA: Allyn & Bacon.

Creighton, Helen. *A Folk Tale Journey*. Wreck Cove, Cape Breton, Nova Scotia, Canada: Breton Books, 1993.

Denning, Stephen. *The Springboard: How Storytelling Ignites Action in Knowledge Era Organizations.* Boston, MA: Butterworth-Heineman, 2001.

Denning, Stephen. *Squirrel Inc.: A Fable of Leadership Through Storytelling.* San Francisco, CA: Jossey-Bass, 2004.

Denning, Stephen. *A Leader's Guide to Storytelling.* San Francisco, CA: Jossey-Bass, 2005.

Dorson, Richard M. *Folk Legends of Japan.* Rutland, VT: Charles E. Tuttle Company, 1962.

Erdoes, Richard, and Ortiz, Alfonso. *American Indian Myths and Legends.* New York: Pantheon, 1984.

Feinstein, David, and Krippner, Stanley. *The Mythic Path.* New York: Tarcher/Putnam, 1997.

Fulford, Robert. *The Triumph of Narrative: Storytelling in the Age of Mass Culture.* New York: Broadway Books, 2001.

Gabriel, Yiannis. *Storytelling in Organizations: Facts, Fictions, and Fantasies.* London: Oxford University Press, 2000.

Gardner, Howard, *Leading Minds: An Anatomy of Leadership.* New York: Basic Books, 1996.

Gargiulo, Terrence L., *Making Stories: A Practical Guide for Organizational Leaders and Human Resource Specialists.* Westport, CT: Greenwood Press, 2002.

Gargiulo, Terrence L. *The Strategic Use of Stories in Organizational Communication and Learning.* Armonk, NY: M.E. Sharpe, 2005.

Gargiulo, Terrence L. *Building Business Acumen for Trainers: Skills to Empower the Learning Function.* San Francsico, CA: Pfeiffer, 2006.

Gargiulo, Terrence L. *Stories at Work: Using Stories to Improve Communication and Build Relationships.* Westport, CT: Praeger, 2006.

Garvin, David A. *Learning in Action: A Guide to Putting the Learning Organization to Work.* Boston, MA: Harvard Business School Press, 2000.

Hale, Judith. *Outsourcing Training and Development: Factors for Success.* San Francisco, CA: Pfeiffer, 2006.

Hillman, James. *A Blue Fire.* New York: Harpers, 1991.

Jensen, Bill. *Simplicty: The New Competitive Advantage in a World of More, Better, Faster.* Cambridge, MA: Perseus Books, 2000.

Lipman, Doug. *Improving Your Storytelling: Beyond the Basics for All Who Tell Stories in Work or Play.* Little Rock, AR: August House: 1999.

Maguire, Jack. *The Power of Personal Storytelling: Spinning Tales to Connect with Others.* New York: Tarcher/Putnam, 1998.

Meade, Erica Helm. *Tell It By Heart: Women and the Healing Power of Story.* Chicago, IL: Open Court, 1995.

Moore, Thomas. *Dark Nights of the Soul.* New York: Gotham, 2005.

Morgan, Gareth. *Imaginization: New Mindsets for Seeing, Organizing, and Managing.* Thousand Oaks, CA: Sage, 1993.

Neuhauser, Peg C. *Corporate Legends and Lore: The Power of Storytelling As a Management Tool.* New York: McGraw-Hill, 1993.

Norgaard, Mette. *The Ugly Duckling Goes to Work.* New York: AMACOM, 2005.

Owens, H. *Open Space Technology: A User's Guide.* San Francisco, CA: Berrett-Koehler, 1997.

Parkin, Margaret. *Tales for Trainers: Using Stories and Metaphors to Facilitate Learning.* London: Kogan Page, 1998.

Parkin, Margaret. *Tales for Change: Using Storytelling to Develop People and Management.* London: Kogan Page, 2004.

Patterson, Kerry, Paterson, Joseph, Grenny, Ron, McMillan, Al, and Parkin, Margaret. *Tales for Coaching: Using Stories and Metaphors with Individuals and Small Groups.* London: Kogan Page, 2001.

Sawyer, Ruth. *The Way of the Storyteller.* New York: Penguin Books, 1976.

Schank, Roger. *Tell Me a Story: A New Look at Real and Artificial Memory.* Chicago, IL: Northwestern University Press, 1995.

Schank, Roger. *Virtual Learning: A Revolutionary Approach to Building a Highly Skilled Workforce.* New York: McGraw-Hill, 1997.

Senge, P. *The Fifth Discipline.* New York: Doubleday, 1990.

Silberman, Mel (Ed.). *Handbook of Experiential Learning.* San Francisco, CA: Pfeiffer: 2007.

Silberman, Mel, and Auerbach, Carol. *Active Training: A Handbook of Techniques, Designs, Case Examples, and Tips* (3rd ed.). San Francisco, CA: Pfeiffer, 2006.

Silberman, Mel, and Hansburg, Freda. *PeopleSmart: Developing Your Interpersonal Intelligence.* San Francisco, CA: Jossey-Bass, 2005.

Silverman, Lori L. *Wake Me Up When the Data Is Over: How Organizations Use Stories to Drive Results.* San Francisco, CA: Jossey-Bass, 2007.

Simons, Annette. *The Story Factor.* Cambridge, MA: Perseus, 2001.

Stolovitch, Harold. *Telling Ain't Training.* Arlington, VA: ASTD, 2002.

Stolovitch, Harold. *Training Ain't Performance.* Arlington, VA: ASTD, 2004.

Stone, Richard. *The Healing Art of Storytelling: A Sacred Journey of Personal Discovery.* New York: Hyperion, 1996.

Switzler, Al. *Crucial Conversations: Tools for Talking When the Stakes Are High.* New York: McGraw-Hill, 2002.

Tichy, Noel M., with Eli Cohen. *The Leadership Engine: How Winning Companies Build Leaders at Every Level.* New York: HarperCollins, 1997.

Wacker, Mary B., and Silverman, Lori L. *Stories Trainers Tell: 55 Ready-To Use Stories to Make Training Stick.* San Francisco, CA: Pfeiffer, 2003.

Wendover, Robert, and Gargiulo, Terrence. *On Cloud Nine: Weathering Generational Challenges in the Workplace.* New York: AMACOM, 2005.

Wheatley, M., and Kellner-Rogers, M. *A Simpler Way.* San Francisco, CA: Berrett-Koehler, 1996.

White, Daniel, and Goldsmith, Marshall. *Guiding People Who Guide Others.* San Francisco, CA: Jossey Bass, 2005.

Wolkstein, Diane. *The Magic Orange Tree and Other Haitian Folktales.* New York: Schocken Books, 1978.

Zeitlin, Steve. *Because God Loves Stories: An Anthology of Jewish Storytelling.* New York: Touchstone, 1997.

Some Parting Thoughts

*A*s I sat in a café reviewing the copy-edited manuscript, I felt impelled to share the following last thoughts with you.

Stories fold in and out of themselves to reveal subtle worlds of meanings, purpose, and connections.

Stories are gentle transporters bound by time but that travel beyond the boundaries of what we have experienced at any given point in time.

Stories free us to move through a landscape of change. We leave the dusty road of the familiar and embrace a void where we can find the freedom to choose and perceive new realities and project worlds of our own making.

Stories can either crush words we have become enslaved to due to habit or they can lift our veils of fear and familiarity and give us a glimpse of new ways of being. Here we will find a place where we can be our unique selves while in communion with others.

Good luck on your journey. Share what you discover with others in the form of stories and encourage them to relish their journeys.

Warmest regards,

About the Author

Terrence L. Gargiulo has spent over fifteen years as an executive coach and group process facilitator. He has been helping people acquire the skills they need to excel as communicators and build successful relationships. He holds a master of management in human services degree from the Florence Heller School at Brandeis University and is a recipient of *Inc.* magazine's Marketing Master Award. He is co-founder of the STORI Institute, where theory, research, and practice meet in the field of stories and narrative.

Among his past and present clients are GM, DTE Energy, Dreyer's Grand Ice Cream, HP, UnumProvident, the U.S. Coast Guard, Boston University, Raytheon, the City of Lowell, Arthur D. Little, KANA Communications, Merck-Medco, Coca-Cola, Harvard Business School, and Cambridge Savings Bank.

His previous books include *Making Stories: A Practical Guide for Organizational Leaders and Human Resource Specialists* (also translated into Chinese); *The Strategic Use of Stories in Organizational Communication and Learning; On Cloud Nine: Weathering Many Generations in the Workplace* (with Robert Wendover; also translated into Korean and Spanish); *Stories at Work: Using Stories to Improve Communications and Relationship;* and *Building Business Acumen for Trainers: Skills to Empower the Learning Function.*

He is a frequent speaker at the international and national conferences of such organizations as the American Society for Training and Development (ASTD), Conference Board, International Society for Performance Improvement (ISPI), Academy of Management, and Association of Business Communications, and he is a field editor for ASTD. His articles have appeared in *American Executive* magazine, *Communication World, Journal of Performance Improvement, Journal of Quality and Participation,* and *ASTD Links.*

Terrence and his father's opera, *Tryillias,* was accepted for a nomination for the 2004 Pulitzer Prize in music. He resides in Monterey, California, and can be reached by phone at 781–894–4381 or e-mail at Terrence@MAKINGTORIES.net. He also has two websites: www.makingstories.net and www.oncloudnine.org.

A Gift from My Father

There is always a story behind the story. As I write this, my ninety-one-year-old father nears the end of his life. I will spend my life reflecting on all of the wonderful stories he has given me. The magic I have tried to re-create in this book is a testament to his art as a conductor and composer. Exceptional facilitation of breakthrough communication is like orchestrating the intricate dynamics of a piece of music. While I have not followed in my father's path as a conductor, I feel his gifts and powers of connecting music, with the hearts of people alive and pulsing in every cell of my being. Mille grazie, Mio Padre. I will never stop trying to create something new from my being each and every moment and you will be there always as my inspiration.

Original manuscript from Maestro Theodore Gargiulo's opera *Tryillias*—"Artban's Aria." A full copy of the engraved aria can found on the CD-ROM accompanying this book or at www.makingstories.net/opera/opera.htm.

How to Use the CD-ROM

System Requirements

PC with Microsoft Windows 98SE or later
Mac with Apple OS version 8.6 or later

Using the CD With Windows

To view the items located on the CD, follow these steps:

1. Insert the CD into your computer's CD-ROM drive.
2. A window appears with the following options:

   Contents: Allows you to view the files included on the CD-ROM.

   Software: Allows you to install useful software from the CD-ROM.

   Links: Displays a hyperlinked page of websites.

   Author: Displays a page with information about the Author(s).

   Contact Us: Displays a page with information on contacting the publisher or author.

   Help: Displays a page with information on using the CD.

   Exit: Closes the interface window.

If you do not have autorun enabled, or if the autorun window does not appear, follow these steps to access the CD:

1. Click Start ⇨ Run.
2. In the dialog box that appears, type d:<\\>start.exe, where d is the letter of your CD-ROM drive. This brings up the autorun window described in the preceding set of steps.
3. Choose the desired option from the menu. (See Step 2 in the preceding list for a description of these options.)

In Case of Trouble

If you experience difficulty using the CD-ROM, please follow these steps:

1. Make sure your hardware and systems configurations conform to the systems requirements noted under "System Requirements" above.

2. Review the installation procedure for your type of hardware and operating system.

It is possible to reinstall the software if necessary.

To speak with someone in Product Technical Support, call 800–762–2974 or 317–572–3994 M–F 8:30 a.m. – 5:00 p.m. EST. You can also get support and contact Product Technical Support through our website at www.wiley.com/techsupport.

Before calling or writing, please have the following information available:

- Type of computer and operating system
- Any error messages displayed
- Complete description of the problem.

It is best if you are sitting at your computer when making the call.

Pfeiffer Publications Guide

This guide is designed to familiarize you with the various types of Pfeiffer publications. The formats section describes the various types of products that we publish; the methodologies section describes the many different ways that content might be provided within a product. We also provide a list of the topic areas in which we publish.

FORMATS

In addition to its extensive book-publishing program, Pfeiffer offers content in an array of formats, from fieldbooks for the practitioner to complete, ready-to-use training packages that support group learning.

FIELDBOOK Designed to provide information and guidance to practitioners in the midst of action. Most fieldbooks are companions to another, sometimes earlier, work, from which its ideas are derived; the fieldbook makes practical what was theoretical in the original text. Fieldbooks can certainly be read from cover to cover. More likely, though, you'll find yourself bouncing around following a particular theme, or dipping in as the mood, and the situation, dictate.

HANDBOOK A contributed volume of work on a single topic, comprising an eclectic mix of ideas, case studies, and best practices sourced by practitioners and experts in the field.

An editor or team of editors usually is appointed to seek out contributors and to evaluate content for relevance to the topic. Think of a handbook not as a ready-to-eat meal, but as a cookbook of ingredients that enables you to create the most fitting experience for the occasion.

RESOURCE Materials designed to support group learning. They come in many forms: a complete, ready-to-use exercise (such as a game); a comprehensive resource on one topic (such as conflict management) containing a variety of methods and approaches; or a collection of like-minded activities (such as icebreakers) on multiple subjects and situations.

TRAINING PACKAGE An entire, ready-to-use learning program that focuses on a particular topic or skill. All packages comprise a guide for the facilitator/trainer and a workbook for the participants. Some packages are supported with additional media—such as video—or learning aids, instruments, or other devices to help participants understand concepts or practice and develop skills.

- *Facilitator/trainer's guide* Contains an introduction to the program, advice on how to organize and facilitate the learning event, and step-by-step instructor notes. The guide also contains copies of presentation materials—handouts, presentations, and overhead designs, for example—used in the program.

- *Participant's workbook* Contains exercises and reading materials that support the learning goal and serves as a valuable reference and support guide for participants in the weeks and months that follow the learning event. Typically, each participant will require his or her own workbook.

ELECTRONIC CD-ROMs and web-based products transform static Pfeiffer content into dynamic, interactive experiences. Designed to take advantage of the searchability, automation, and ease-of-use that technology provides, our e-products bring convenience and immediate accessibility to your workspace.

METHODOLOGIES

CASE STUDY A presentation, in narrative form, of an actual event that has occurred inside an organization. Case studies are not prescriptive, nor are they used to prove a point; they are designed to develop critical analysis and decision-making skills. A case study has a specific time frame, specifies a sequence of events, is narrative in structure, and contains a plot structure—an issue (what should be/have been done?). Use case studies when the goal is to enable participants to apply previously learned theories to the circumstances in the case, decide what is pertinent, identify the real issues, decide what should have been done, and develop a plan of action.

ENERGIZER A short activity that develops readiness for the next session or learning event. Energizers are most commonly used after a break or lunch to stimulate or refocus the group. Many involve some form of physical activity, so they are a useful way to counter post-lunch lethargy. Other uses include transitioning from one topic to another, where "mental" distancing is important.

EXPERIENTIAL LEARNING ACTIVITY (ELA) A facilitator-led intervention that moves participants through the learning cycle from experience to application (also known as a Structured Experience). ELAs are carefully thought-out designs in which there is a definite learning purpose and intended outcome. Each step—everything that participants do during the activity—facilitates the accomplishment of the stated goal. Each ELA includes complete instructions for facilitating the intervention and a clear statement of goals, suggested group size and timing, materials required, an explanation of the process, and, where appropriate, possible variations to the activity. (For more detail on Experiential Learning Activities, see the Introduction to the *Reference Guide to Handbooks and Annuals*, 1999 edition, Pfeiffer, San Francisco.)

GAME A group activity that has the purpose of fostering team spirit and togetherness in addition to the achievement of a pre-stated goal. Usually contrived—undertaking a desert expedition, for example—this type of learning method offers an engaging means for participants to demonstrate and practice business and interpersonal skills. Games are effective for team building and personal development mainly because the goal is subordinate to the process—the means through which participants reach decisions, collaborate, communicate, and generate trust and understanding. Games often engage teams in "friendly" competition.

ICEBREAKER A (usually) short activity designed to help participants overcome initial anxiety in a training session and/or to acquaint the participants with one another. An icebreaker can be a fun activity or can be tied to specific topics or training goals. While a useful tool in itself, the icebreaker comes into its own in situations where tension or resistance exists within a group.

INSTRUMENT A device used to assess, appraise, evaluate, describe, classify, and summarize various aspects of human behavior. The term used to describe an instrument depends primarily on its format and purpose. These terms include survey, questionnaire, inventory, diagnostic, survey, and poll. Some uses of instruments include providing instrumental feedback to group members, studying here-and-now processes or functioning within a group, manipulating group composition, and evaluating outcomes of training and other interventions.

Instruments are popular in the training and HR field because, in general, more growth can occur if an individual is provided with a method for focusing specifically on his or her own behavior. Instruments also are used to obtain information that will serve as a basis for change and to assist in workforce planning efforts.

Paper-and-pencil tests still dominate the instrument landscape with a typical package comprising a facilitator's guide, which offers advice on administering the instrument and interpreting the collected data, and an initial set of instruments. Additional instruments are available separately. Pfeiffer, though, is investing heavily in e-instruments. Electronic instrumentation provides effortless distribution and, for larger groups particularly, offers advantages over paper-and-pencil tests in the time it takes to analyze data and provide feedback.

LECTURETTE A short talk that provides an explanation of a principle, model, or process that is pertinent to the participants' current learning needs. A lecturette is intended to establish a common language bond between the trainer and the participants by providing a mutual frame of reference. Use a lecturette as an introduction to a group activity or event, as an interjection during an event, or as a handout.

MODEL A graphic depiction of a system or process and the relationship among its elements. Models provide a frame of reference and something more tangible, and more easily remembered, than a verbal explanation. They also give participants something to "go on," enabling them to track their own progress as they experience the dynamics, processes, and relationships being depicted in the model.

ROLE PLAY A technique in which people assume a role in a situation/scenario: a customer service rep in an angry-customer exchange, for example. The way in which the role is approached is then discussed and feedback is offered. The role play is often repeated using a different approach and/or incorporating changes made based on feedback received. In other words, role playing is a spontaneous interaction involving realistic behavior under artificial (and safe) conditions.

SIMULATION A methodology for understanding the interrelationships among components of a system or process. Simulations differ from games in that they test or use a model that depicts or mirrors some aspect of reality in form, if not necessarily in content. Learning occurs by studying the effects of change on one or more factors of the model. Simulations are commonly used to test hypotheses about what happens in a system—often referred to as "what if?" analysis—or to examine best-case/worst-case scenarios.

THEORY A presentation of an idea from a conjectural perspective. Theories are useful because they encourage us to examine behavior and phenomena through a different lens.

TOPICS

The twin goals of providing effective and practical solutions for workforce training and organization development and meeting the educational needs of training and human resource professionals shape Pfeiffer's publishing program. Core topics include the following:

Leadership & Management

Communication & Presentation

Coaching & Mentoring

Training & Development

E-Learning

Teams & Collaboration

OD & Strategic Planning

Human Resources

Consulting

What will you find on pfeiffer.com?

- The best in workplace performance solutions for training and HR professionals

- Downloadable training tools, exercises, and content

- Web-exclusive offers

- Training tips, articles, and news

- Seamless on-line ordering

- Author guidelines, information on becoming a Pfeiffer Affiliate, and much more

Discover more at www.pfeiffer.com